The Gove[nment] Mani[festo] t

Disruptive Governance thinking for the masses

Ant Clay

The SharePoint Governance Manifesto

Disruptive Governance thinking for the masses

Ant Clay

This book is for sale at
http://leanpub.com/The-SharePoint-Governance-Manifesto

This version was published on 2013-07-10

ISBN 978-0-9575801-3-8

SOULSAILOR
CONSULTING

This is a Leanpub book, generated using the Lean Publishing process. Lean Publishing is the act of publishing an in-progress ebook using lightweight tools and many iterations to get reader feedback, pivot until you have the right book and build traction once you do.

Published By **Soulsailor Consulting Ltd**

Tweet This Book!

Please help Ant Clay by spreading the word about this book on Twitter!

The suggested hashtag for this book is #SPGovManifesto.

Find out what other people are saying about the book by clicking on this link to search for this hashtag on Twitter:

https://twitter.com/search/#SPGovManifesto

Contents

CONTENTS

Dedicated to...

My wife Claire for always being here to "steer me" on the right path.

My awesome kids Rowan, Flynn and Erin for your sheer honesty, playful insights and constant support.

Credits and Thanks

I really appreciate the immense positivity, help, support, feedback and inspiration from everyone I know on Twitter, LinkedIn, Facebook and within the awesome global SharePoint community, for this my first, very tenuous step, into becoming an author.

I want to especially thank the tireless reviewers who shared with me their advice, experience and a real dose of pragmatism when I most needed it!

This book really wouldn't be what it is today without you guys: Andy Talbot (@SharePointAndy), Jim Anning (@JimAnning), Joe Capka (@JCapka), Jon Maunder (@Jon_Maunder), Nancy Skaggs (@NanSkatoon), Paul Hunt (@Cimares), Richard Martin, Seb Matthews (@SebMatthews), Nigel Price (@Nigel_Price) and John Timney (@JTimney).

And finally, sincere thanks to the 'Constant Doodler' Shaun Cuff http://www.theconstantdoodler.co.uk for the simplicity and beauty of the cover image for this book; you have captured the very essence of Governance in that one single pen-stroke!

Foreword

Christian Buckley (Axceler), SharePoint MVP

Governance planning is a disruptive activity, primarily because not many people know what it is, or how to even begin addressing it in a meaningful way. Add a collaboration platform like SharePoint to the mix, and you have mass confusion. Most people get hung up on the definition. So, what is governance, really?

Governance does not equal administration. Governance is the plan, while administration is the action.

Most SharePoint "experts" abhor the term "best practices" because, practically speaking, what is a best practice for one organization may not be the best practice for others. What makes governance such a difficult topic to define and discuss in general terms is that it may mean different things to different organizations. Most consultants will bring to the table a perspective on governance that closely aligns with their backgrounds: someone with expertise in infrastructure planning and architecture will likely approach governance from an IT assurance perspective. Someone with a background in taxonomy development and business analysis will likely approach it from an information governance standpoint. And there's nothing wrong with these approaches – if they fit the needs of the business. The problem is that few consultants, and the organizations they serve, approach governance holistically.

In his book *The 7 Habits of Highly Effective People* (Covey, 2000, http://bit.ly/Coveys7Habits), Stephen R. Covey identified a principle that has become one of the most oft-repeated phrases in management training: "Seek first to understand, then to be understood." As Covey points out, it is human nature to listen to people and interpret requirements autobiographically. We judge the things we hear and then quickly agree or disagree, we ask questions from our own frame of reference, we jump to solutions, and we assume the motives of other based on our own experiences.

Now apply these same biases to SharePoint governance planning, and you might have some insight into where your own planning efforts may have gone astray. Organizations need to slow down and take the time to talk to end users, managers, and administrators about how SharePoint is being used today (or, if it's a new SharePoint deployment, how current business workloads are being achieved) so that everyone has a shared understanding of what the current system looks like, and ONLY THEN begin the conversation about what the future system should look like. The future system that meets all of your information rights management policies, your regulatory and security requirements, your social connectivity goals, and your content lifecycle strategies.

The benefit of having a clear picture of the current system and an outline of the future system is that you'll have a baseline for conversations around how best to get from here to there.

And that's where governance comes in. Governance is about helping you move from the current view into the future view. It is the plan, the policies and guidelines, to help you cross that void, to fill that gap.

What I love about the book that Ant has compiled here is that it aligns perfectly with this philosophy. His approach, influenced by the work he did with Andrew Woodward at 21apps, and industry experts such as Paul Culmsee and others, begins with the idea that you cannot move forward successfully without having a "shared vision" for what your SharePoint platform wants to be when it grows up. All of the other governance "best practices" stem from this one point, whether it be the creation of a governance Centre of Excellence, implementation of detailed SharePoint change management protocols, or the inclusion of a detailed end user training plan, including mentoring program (all of which I highly recommend). All good things, but all reliant on that shared vision – at least if you want them to meaningful and long-lasting.

This book will help you to think more about your own approach to solving the SharePoint governance challenge, and to figure out what will work best for your own organization. Take what makes sense, and is applicable, and make it your own. Ask questions. Reach out to Ant and others within the community for answers. You have a great support system already in place, no matter where you are in the world. Good luck!

Prelude

User Guide

If you thought from the cover image that it was about sailing, then sorry it's not, although it does get a mention.

This book is about the challenges, impact and approaches to implementing SharePoint Governance in your organisation.

When I say SharePoint what do I really mean? SharePoint, hosted SharePoint and SharePoint Online for sure. The reality is that, although the basis of this book is Microsoft SharePoint, it is actually also relevant to any other social or collaborative platform (Yammer, IBM Lotus Connections, Jive, Huddle, etc.) that you and your organisation may be using.

Actually, there's a lot you can take from this book and apply to the Governance of pretty much anything!

I wrote this Manifesto to be three things for you:

1. **Disruptive** because the status quo really isn't delivering
2. **Thought provoking** because none of this is easy
3. **Informative** for both you and your organisation.

The disruption comes from the early chapters where we will "Poke the Box" as Seth Godin would say (Godin, 2011 http://bit.ly/PokeSeth) and highlight our challenges with Governance itself.

The mid-section of this book is more visual and questioning. It illustrates key points, both positive and negative, about our perceptions and the future of SharePoint Governance.

Finally, in the last section, we focus on being informative in a positively disruptive way. We will explore how you can apply my '7 **Waves of Governance**' in your organisation and projects. An approach to Governance which has been developed over the last 4 years and successfully implemented with a range of clients from

SME to global organisations, as well as within a number of Microsoft partners. We will consider in detail how this approach works and the significant benefits of implementing and embedding SharePoint Governance within your organisation. The combination of these insights and approaches will, I hope, be informative, engaging and offer practical advice that will help you deliver organisational value by positively disrupting your technology projects.

State of the community

When I asked the SharePoint Twitter community what they perceived as SharePoint Governance, this is a sample of what people told me:

> "I think governance starts when some [one] with a lot of pull says, Man! This is crazy!"
> - **Stacy Draper (@StacyDraper)**

> "abused term defined differently depending on who you ask"
> - **Andrew Clark (@SharePointAC)**

> "Good SharePoint governance starts with an IM strategy"
> **- Alan Pelze-Sharpe (@AlanPelzeSharpe) **

> "gov = organizational & management environment defining accountability & responsibility 4 return on SP investment"
> - **Symon Garfield (@Symon_Garfield)**

"The G word that Allows, Controls, Denies, Defines, Dictates, Enables, Governs, Innovates, Promotes, Promises and Delivers :)"
- Dave Heron (@Davipops)

"Governance = Rules to tell us what we should or should not do outside the ways the technology itself limits us"
- Marc Anderson (@SympMarc)

"The thing you're not doing, that you know you should be doing. :(:)"
- Art Ho (Art_Ho)

"Governance is about taking action to help your organisation organise, optimise and manage your systems and resource"
- James Fowell (@JFowell)

"Guidelines that provide useful insights into the value that can be delivered to support the business's aspirational state"
- Jon Maunder (@Jon_Maunder)

"SP Governance is like parenting - give them enough rules to keep them safe, & enough flexibility to be creative and grow."
- **Linnea Lewis (@linthecity)**

"SharePoint Governance is a guideline of rules within your organisation, including what, why, when, where and how"
- **Andy Talbot (@SharePointAndy)**

"Governance is not a software or technology problem, it's a people problem"
- **Seb Matthews (@SebMatthews)**

A remarkably divergent set of thoughts and ideas about what is perceived by the community as SharePoint Governance, and on face value a rather confusing set of responses.

This book will shed some light, deliver some clarity and be a comfort to all of you out there wrestling with what SharePoint Governance is, but more importantly is will outline why it matters and how to implement it in your organisation.

Governance versionality

I accept that's not quite a real word, but *versionality* in the context of this manifesto is the state whereby Microsoft (or any other vendor) delivers an exciting new piece of technology, just as you get your head around the current version and have started to focus on the business not the technology.

At the time of writing, SharePoint 2010 is the prevalent version and the next incarnation, SharePoint 2013 has just been released. I've witnessed over the preceding year and a half that the technology community had just started changing the way they work. I was heartened by the fact that it felt like, as a community, we were moving at a quickening pace towards a more business led perspective on SharePoint projects.

But you suddenly changed!

Now, with the water-cooler chats, tweets and blog posts all looking forward to the next version of SharePoint, I fear and I'm already seeing the signs that a large proportion of you SharePoint people have had your heads turned. The shiny new version [it does look good!] is beckoning you with its new features and you have started to veer off-course and back to being SharePoint tech, not business focussed.

You may think that's bad news for me and this manifesto, but no...

Take note SharePoint 2007, 2010, 2013 or vNext+++, or any other damn collaboration platform vendors out there.

Yes I mean you Yammer, Huddle, IBM, DropBox and SAP!

You all need Governance, this manifesto is timeless, or at least I hope it will be and I'll be waiting for the SharePoint vNext excitement to die down and a new business focussed normality to return.

Governance lasts forever...

I hope you'll join me on this kick-ass road-trip disrupting Governance thinking...

Why?

Why did I write this book?

I'm sure you can't have helped but notice the huge amount of Governance content out there? There are blogs, videos, slides, tweets, status updates and water-cooler conversations to name just a few common sources. It's an absolute minefield for anyone new, trying to fathom out what the hell SharePoint Governance is, what it means to them and what the dire consequences are if they don't do anything about it soon.

Why would I want to write this manifesto about SharePoint Governance?

Why would I think it was a good idea to deliver "Disruptive Governance thinking for the masses"?

One reason is that I want to put a very clear stake into the ground about what Governance really is. My personal perspective is based on many years of using and implementing collaborative technology platforms across a range of sectors. Just like you, I have been stumbling through the Governance challenges that most, if not all organisations have with this type of solution. I really wanted to distil and articulate how you can practically deliver a holistic Governance approach within your organisation.

Lastly, I want to make a difference.

I want to make a disruptive, bold, emotional, arse-kicking, blinding-light kind of difference...

Whether that's even possible with a subject like SharePoint Governance I don't know, time will tell, but that is very much my 'big hairy audacious goal' (Collins & Jerry, 1994, http://bit.ly/BigHairyAudaciousGoal).

Simply put, I want to enable you all to deliver value to your organisations. I propose to do this by disrupting your SharePoint projects with the words, experiences, analogies, tools and techniques that are contained within this manifesto...

I hope that this book will cut through all the existing SharePoint Governance crap that is out there and steer you on a path to SharePoint awesomeness.

What is this crazy thing called Governance?

Well at a very simple level, it's all about putting things, but not necessarily just large documents and overbearing rules, in place that help your project achieve its vision or goal. Put another way, Governance helps to ensure that your project can actually start to deliver the difference it should make to your business.

The word *Governance*, as stated in Wikipedia, is said to have been derived from the Greek verb Kubernáo, used for the first time in a metaphorical sense by Plato.

In Latin, the term Governance means '**To Steer**' and this is my seminal definition, first imparted to me by the famed Australian SharePoint and collaboration sensemaker, Paul Culmsee (http://bit.ly/Culmsee).

It was this insight that brought clarity to my already business-focussed perspective of Governance. It's also pretty convenient for me that Governance can be grounded in the nautical steer theme, as I am an avid sailor!

Take a look at the statements below, are these concepts that you can see within your organisation?

- A SharePoint Vision
- Stories about SharePoint making a difference
- A SharePoint Business Case
- SharePoint Return on Investment
- Measurable SharePoint Business Outcomes.

Ask yourself this:

Do you really deliver these things to your stake-holders and users?

Do you think perhaps Governance could be part of the answer?

I Do.

Why are SharePoint projects so complex?

My experience, over the last decade is that in way too many instances, SharePoint projects fail to deliver true business value. They're delivered as though they are just another Microsoft Office productivity solution, implemented as a technology project with a huge and catastrophic assumption that "If you build it, they will come" (Field of Dreams, 1989).

Dave Snowden's 'Cynefin Framework' (Snowden, 2012 http://bit.ly/Cynefin) is immensely useful in sensemaking the complexity of delivering collaborative and social solutions, such as SharePoint, to my clients. I apply the Cynefin Framework to demonstrate why we can't just assume that a technology solution on its own will deliver value and solve our organisations business problems.

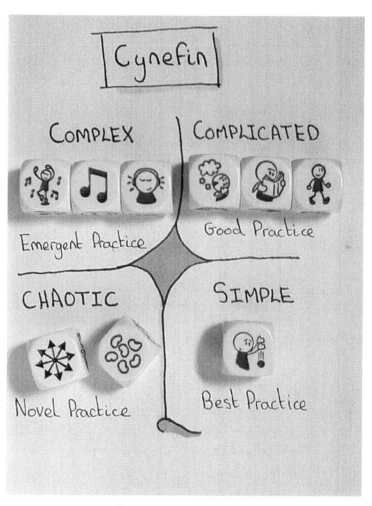

Cynefin Framework sketch

Originally developed in the context of knowledge management and organisational strategy, *'Cynefin'*, a welsh word, literally translated to mean *'habitat, or place of multiple belongings'*, is now applied in many diverse ways, including complex adaptive systems, decision-making, cultural change, organisational strategy and community dynamics.

As you can see in the previous sketch, we have a typical four quadrant diagram, with each quadrant sensemaking particular scenarios, one of which I feel is most appropriate to SharePoint and collaborative or knowledge management projects.

In the **Simple quadrant**, life is very much cause and effect. As you can see by the character, every time they drop the ball it falls to the ground, that action is infinitely repeatable with the same predictable effect.

Have you ever implemented a SharePoint solution that you could repeat in any team, company, or sector that would always have the same repeatable and predictable cause and effect?

Nope, I didn't think so!

So SharePoint, collaboration and knowledge management solutions don't live here in this quadrant.

> **You know all the focus in SharePoint land on 'Best Practice'?**
>
> **It's an oxymoron.**
>
> **Think about that for a second...**

Moving up to the **Complicated quadrant**, this is where the previously simple and repeatable relationship between cause and effect requires investigation, analysis or the application of expert knowledge in order to be effective. Here we can see from our characters that an expert is analysing the situation, the consultant character is reading about that knowledge and implementing a solution influenced by that thinking. The result being the end user character is walking away happily. Now we may see this kind of behaviour in more infrastructure based projects such as Microsoft Exchange, but not for collaboration, knowledge management and SharePoint scenarios. True, most technology projects are implemented as 'good practice' or even worse perhaps using 'best practice', but if we analyse those projects we will see that the projects are deemed failures because they do not deliver the outcomes required by the business.

What I have found, in my experience, is that projects delivered with the assumption that the business problem they are solving is in the 'Complicated' or 'Simple' domain, although outwardly they do fail, they do make some positive steps towards the goal. The challenge is that the implementers, very often do not see things with a perspective of learning and continuous improvement and therefore the one-shot project cannot hope to capitalise on the value that has already been delivered.

Now things get interesting in the **Complex quadrant**. As you can see from the characters, we have music playing in the background and we have two emergent behaviours:

1. The first person is dancing
2. The second person is listening intently.

Both characters are happy and are deriving value from the music in different ways, perhaps ways we had not imagined or expected. From a Cynefin perspective the relationship between cause and effect is only perceived in retrospect, never in advance. For our characters, that implies that depending on whom they are, what they are doing and even their mood, different behaviours will emerge from the same music playing.

In terms of our work around SharePoint Governance, this fits nicely with what we experience every day. We implement a solution based on what the business stakeholders state their requirements are, they use it for some period of time and then we start to hear about the users' unrest:

- It doesn't quite work right
- A particular team "doesn't work like that"
- When I said I wanted this I meant that
- Can you move the search box over there?
- But in this situation, we want it to work like this...

Familiar?

Is that what tends to happen to your SharePoint projects?

What we are seeing are emergent requirements, emergent behaviours and emergent use-cases. Implementing the solution based on what *they* think they want helps the user community to further evolve their understanding of the problem or goal. It is through continuous improvement that we can work with them to evolve the solution to meet their goals.

Finally, for completeness, although a little out of the remit for this book, is the **Chaotic quadrant**. There is no relationship here between cause and effect at a systems level, so behaviour is unpredictable and although at times that may feel true of our SharePoint user community it isn't the reality!

So let us remember, SharePoint projects are people projects and people projects are emergent and therefore they are most definitely not a one shot solution.

A Sailing analogy

I use sailing regularly with clients as a simple analogy for what Governance really means.

Of course if you have any real appreciation of proper sailing, rather than a romantic notion of bobbing along the river (or out on the sea) with a G&T in your hand, then you might just see it as being more like:

> *"standing in the garden while someone throws buckets of cold water at you, while you rip up notes of your favourite currency!"*

But I digress.

What I hope is that you will realise that there's a host of factors that can influence your success in racing a sailing boat around a course. These are in many ways, not dissimilar to SharePoint success factors, and may include:

Having your boat set-up correctly - This is the same concept as having the appropriate SharePoint infrastructure to meet your business needs.

Having a fast boat - Is no different to having appropriate SharePoint performance for what you want to deliver.

Being great at sailing - Having those skills is just the same as having a SharePoint team with great technical skills.

Taking changing weather into consideration - Just as sailors have to change their plans based on the weather, SharePoint Governance needs to flex in order to managing change such as strategy changes, technology change, project constraints etc.

Knowing where you are - You may have a vision, but if you don't understand where you are and what you have now then how can you measure progress towards your goal?

Awareness of obstacles (other boats, shore and obstructions etc.) - This is just your normal risk management, but it's an important element of on-going SharePoint governance.

Steering the boat the right way - Well that's what we are talking about, that's your SharePoint Governance!

As you can see the analogy of sailing holds water (excuse the pun) for SharePoint Governance. Also, for some IT stakeholders you may know or maybe even you, implementing SharePoint may well feel very similar to the experience of sailing.

Perhaps this is a familiar feeling?

> *"Standing in a server room while the business throws buckets of cold water and your IT team rip up notes of your favourite currency from your budget..."*

Sailing is therefore, clearly a similar process to designing, implementing and maintaining your SharePoint platform. We must always remember though, that to be successful at sailing you have to focus continually on all these aspects listed above (and more), so let's look at the negative consequences of only focusing on one of those facets?

I'm a great Sailor, years of experience:

I'm sailing faster than the competition, but I'm sailing fast, in the wrong direction, I don't follow the right course, I miss out marks, I get disqualified!

I'm an awesome tactician:

Tactically I'm sailing really well, but I'm not looking at where the wind is and everyone is sailing faster than me and I didn't notice that island...bump...sink...FAIL!

I have a fast boat:

My boat is the newest, most expensive, fastest and full of go-faster gadgets, but I don't know how to sail very well, the sails are flapping and I'm not sure where I'm going.... the boat goes very slowly, I didn't finish the race, I'm not a winner!

As I hope you can see in sailing, just focusing on getting one thing right isn't going to guarantee you success, just as in our SharePoint world, it's exactly the same challenge.

I'll explain this cause and effect scenario a whole lot more when I talk in detail about the "The 7 Waves of Governance".

Beware of Governance snake-oil

Why does SharePoint Governance deserve my focus for this manifesto?

It is because I think that SharePoint Governance is completely screwed!

Maybe that's a little strong, but basically everyone has an opinion about what Governance means and how you should apply it, including:

- Your IT department
- Microsoft
- Tool vendors
- SharePoint MVP's
- Your boss
- Microsoft Partners
- Consultants
- Business stakeholders
- And of course you!

Yes, when it comes down to it, anyone that has anything to do with SharePoint is probably selling some kind of Governance snake-oil (opinion, tools, frameworks etc.) to yourself, your team or worse to the business stakeholders in your organisation, looking for answers.

The challenge is that I honestly think you and the rest of them are all just a little bit wrong...

Yes that is very bold statement, but there is very little convergent thinking around Governance at the moment and most of what I see and hear in organisations has some serious flaws.

Perhaps I am being too harsh, but that's just the way I see it based on my experiences.

The challenge is that:

- Microsoft is selling their technology
- Microsoft Partners are selling their consulting
- Tool vendors are selling their tools
- And so on.

All these groups of people have valid insights into Governance, but they are also falling foul of their company's world-views and KPI's (Key Performance Indicators), which are always grounded on selling more of their stuff.

I truly believe that individuals across the SharePoint community and wider collaboration, knowledge management and sensemaking spaces have a huge amount to offer in terms of governance thinking and frameworks, but we need to more explicitly anchor these thoughts with business Governance ideals.

If my thinking and bold statements don't sit well with you, then let me know why. SharePoint will never be confined to just one person, it's a team sport, its community supported and dare I say it, collaborative. It's my hope that we can be on the same page and together change SharePoint Governance forever in a positive way!

How do we achieve this?

Well a starting point will be for us all to share our Governance experiences with the community. Both the wider SharePoint community and the community that I hope will form around this book.

If you experience change (hopefully positive) and value from approaching SharePoint Governance differently, based on the ideals and approaches articulated within this book, then please share.

All feedback is welcomed, embraced and will quite probably be the basis for future Governance work and publications!

Let us not forget that SharePoint Governance needs to be collaborative!

This book is not Governance snake-oil, this is a new way of Governance thinking...

Why Governance is failing

Why is Governance failing?

What is continually catching us out?

Here are my top 10 reasons:

1. Microsoft are selling (extremely well) technology.
2. Our thinking has historically pivoted around what IT can achieve.
3. We still think technology tools will save us.
4. Governance is a platitude.
5. Governance is a wicked problem (Rittel, P. H., 2012, http://bit.ly/WickedProblem).
6. It seems to be way too much hard work to implement this Governance thing.
7. SharePoint is huge, who is responsible for Governance?
8. The world is full of divergent thinking.
9. SharePoint projects are complex according to the Cynefin Framework (Snowden, 2012, http://bit.ly/Cynefin).
10. SharePoint projects are implemented as technology projects when really they should be defined as change projects.

Another way to look at why SharePoint Governance is so important and needs this manifesto is that most SharePoint projects I've seen, despite the rhetoric and case studies, have fundamentally failed.

The Governance we thought we knew all about and had implemented isn't saving our project's arse.

When I say that most SharePoint projects are failing, let me clarify what I mean. I accept that as far as the project plan, user testing, project team and even the business case are concerned (you do have one don't you?) the project may have been deemed a success. However, when you look at the deliverables and the actual difference the project has made to the business, my experience is that most projects deliver very little measurable business value.

In fact what they deliver is what I politely call a pile of celery, SharePoint Celery to be specific and that surely isn't what we are striving for is it?

The celery effect

Let me explain what I mean.

According to nutritionists the average stick of celery can give us about 8 calories in nutritional value. Whereas the physical act of picking up the celery, eating it and digesting it actually uses around 14 calories...

Eating celery gives you a negative calorific value, it's basically pointless unless you are trying to lose weight and become healthier, which I am, but that's not the point of this anecdote.

Now let's compare eating celery with implementing a SharePoint project.

Let's be very honest and add up the real cost of a project:

- Infrastructure
- Licenses
- Project time
- Business time in the project for requirements gathering and testing
- User training time etc.

If we compared that to the demonstrable business value generated by the project, I suspect in way too many cases that aren't just platform implementations, the costs outweigh the value, giving a negative Return on Investment (ROI).

So you should now see that implementing SharePoint in an inappropriate way, without proper Governance and without aligning it to business needs and vision, is the same as eating celery; it's no good, and there's no value in it.

So stop eating Celery.

Stop implementing SharePoint Celery Projects.

Implement proper SharePoint Governance.

Do SharePoint for the businesses sake.

Do stay healthy, have a balanced diet and exercise some more!

How the hell did it get so bad?

B. A. Baracus, was a legendary TV character, pivotal to the success of the TV series 'The A Team', his death...

Oops! Sorry, wrong BA!

At the time of writing he's thankfully not dead, although he is making very questionable chocolate bar adverts.

I want to start, not by lamenting old TV series characters, but by examining the demise of the Business Analyst (BA), or to be more precise the demise of what I refer to as the *analyst paradigm*.

Back in 1999, at the dawn of the mainstream adoption of the Intranet, when Lotus Notes was emerging as the dominant player and Microsoft hadn't even joined the party, a fundamental shift occurred in Information Technology that I believe we all completely missed.

Let me justify my wild statement, before you throw the book away in disgust and let's add some context to this...

Before the arrival of IT beasts like our present day corporate Intranet, things were different.

Technology was the innovative force in the business world, driving businesses to change the way it worked, trust emerged in what technology could do and how it could improve task-based efficiencies.

Software was used effectively to replicate and improve upon human and paper-based actions and tasks.

Our technology solutions were focussed on enablement and delivering efficiencies that we humans alone couldn't achieve.

Back in the day, the role of the IT professional was to analyse human activities, work out how technology could do tasks faster, more effectively, make less mistakes and then we wrote some code and created an application that did exactly that, replacing human tasks.

Life was (relatively) easy and technology made a fundamental but very predictable difference to our day to day lives.

Governance was all about controlling those new technology beasts we had created and making sure they did our bidding with no unpredictable consequences.

Then technology matured, we started to delve into web technologies and new concepts inside the boundary of our firewalls and the corporate bricks and mortar and this thing called a 'corporate Intranet' was born, supposedly to help us become 'amazingly effective' in our day-to-day work.

And why did we pin such high and lofty expectations on another emergent technology concept? It was because the way we use technology was evolving frighteningly rapidly, moving from just replication of human activity to the augmentation of business processes, human interactions and technology into a symbiosis we named the 'corporate intranet'.

We started being able to do more with the assistive support of a new breed of software application solutions than we ever could have achieved with pen and paper or green-screen computing.

This new-found power and desire to do more complex tasks with applications ushered in the new big boy technology companies like Lotus, Microsoft, Oracle, SAP and a load more that have been and gone and I don't remember their names...

As far as I can see, this became the tipping point that, in my opinion everyone in corporate business and IT missed! This was the era when analysing business requirements for application solutions happened in a traditional way, such as:

- Ask questions of the people who shout loudest
- Write some notes
- Go into a darkened room
- Make some (mostly) educated assumptions

- Translate requirements into solution
- Tell the techies what to develop
- Techies deliver your technology solution.

This approach, once simple and effective and still is for more analytical solutions like MS Exchange or infrastructure projects, became very ineffectual in this new world with its rising tide of complexity brought about by:

- Increasing social dynamics
- Problem wickedness (Rittel, 2012, http://bit.ly/WickedProblem)
- Time pressures
- Social complexity
- Technical advancements and maturity.

In fact the change may have started earlier than this, perhaps even way back in 1995 when the 'Chaos Report' (The Standish Group, 1995) was first published, there were signs that people could see the potential issues and challenges in current IT practices:

- Lack of user input
- Incomplete requirements & specifications
- Changing requirements & assumptions
- Lack of executive support
- Unclear objectives.

This was the timely death of the Analyst Paradigm; we didn't get invited to the funeral and we still haven't, for the most part noticed the empty chair in the IT department.

The future of Governance isn't written down

This new world doesn't flow like a waterfall, it's not simple, it's no longer about cause and effect, technology solutions are no longer in the domain of the IT department; it's not about replicating manual processes it's about:

- Adaptive challenges in Business (Heifetz, 2009, http://bit.ly/ AdaptiveHeifetz)
- Human Process Management & Workflows
- Complexity Theory
- Peoples Experience and Judgment
- Collaborative outcomes
- Social business
- Continuous Improvement.

The old analyst paradigm we discussed in the previous section just doesn't make any sense anymore... It is broken, completely borked, irreconcilable, forever lost.

Well at least it should be, but it seems far too many of us in IT, actually scratch that, in IT AND business, are still wedded to this ineffective analyst paradigm.

This really does have to stop right now!

I'm guessing that from that disruption emerges questions similar to this:

> If I'm not going to write a requirements spread-sheet and 100 page Governance documents any-more, how on earth are we going to do software projects?
>
> We're not going to do software projects anymore.

The technology project ship has passed.

We need to change the way we work, have a different vision and learn new skills and techniques.

From this point in time forth, we need to be doing **business projects**, there's no need or in-fact value in mentioning technology in the title, businesses really don't give a crap:

- Document Management
- Financial Portal
- Managers Dashboard
- Social Collaboration
- HR Team Collaboration Site.

The reality is that even those titles above don't really cut it, my view, now more than ever before, with our financial crashes, increasing competition, an evolving workforce and massive complexity is that we need to be stating projects in terms of 'what difference will this make' to our employees and more importantly to our organisation. If we can't define that, then we shouldn't be doing the project, we're just wasting our time on a futile endeavour.

It was once said, in a blog post that I wrote a year or two back that SharePoint Governance should be:

> *"A guiding, facilitative and inclusive approach to implementing the SharePoint platform and delivering measurable business outcomes that support the organisational strategy"*

Let me tell you here, on the pages of this book, that that is exactly what the future of SharePoint Governance and technology projects in general need to look like; that's the change that you have to make and that's the purpose of this book.

But heed this warning.

In this book we are **only** addressing SharePoint Governance, not solving the complexities of organisational Governance. As Nancy Skaggs (http://www.linkedin.com/in/nancyskaggs) comments:

> "..the key problem is (often) that there is no organisational strategy. So how can you craft measurable outcomes? The answer is you cannot."

A final thought on why you should read this book

If you don't read this book and spread the word and we as a SharePoint community don't begin to change the way we think and work, then we will, ad infinitum, continue to fail our organisations and customers and continue to deliver ineffectual, over-bearing, command-and-control, tree-killing, huge tomes of documentation that no-one reads or gains any value from.

I need you to stop talking SharePoint, stop thinking of Governance as the domain of the IT team...

Seriously, do your users give a crap about SharePoint? No of course they don't, they're just trying to stay in a job and feed their family; seriously is SharePoint really more important than that?

No, of course not!

We all need to stop talking about Governance as if it's something new or a magical antidote to all our SharePoint challenges. It isn't at all!

As my SharePoint friend Susan Hanley (http://www.susanhanley.com) said to me at the SHARE2012 SharePoint Business Conference in Atlanta:

> "..Surely good SharePoint Governance is just doing projects the right way?"

Is that a light-bulb moment for you?

It should be and it was for me...

So again, why should you read this book?

Well, the fact that you've read this far means (I hope) that you can (or already could) see the flaws in conventional Governance thinking; if that's the case then at least I have either opened your eyes to the problem or added weight to your hunches or maybe even clarified a thing or two. For the fact that you are another person in the vast global SharePoint community that is on the same page as me, I am truly eternally grateful. Perhaps that is enough of a seed of change?

If it's not, then please continue to read this book, especially if you, your team, business stakeholders and colleagues:

- Are finding your SharePoint projects are failing
- Are feeling there must be a better way
- Want to do SharePoint projects the right way.

As SharePoint Consultants you should live your SharePoint life by this book if you:

- Don't grok (understand) SharePoint Governance at all
- Want your Governance to be read, understood, valued and be worthwhile
- Want to change the way you think
- Decide that fire fighting SharePoint projects wasn't your chosen vocation
- Think that disrupting technology projects sounds a fun past-time!

If that's not enough then thanks for sticking with me this far, I hope I haven't wasted your time, if I have then you're probably one in a million 'cus there's a hell of a lot of people out there who really need this book.

Can I ask that if you're bailing on me at this juncture to sell or give-away this book to someone you know that needs their technology projects disrupting, after all there is a **Share** in **Share**Point!

The Visual Thesis of Kubernáo

Introduction

This next chapter seeks to, in a visual way, be both thought provoking and disruptive, perhaps a challenge for a Governance book but please bear with me!

In the style of the awesome 'Cluetrain Manifesto' (Locke, et al., 2000, http://bit.ly/TheCluetrainManifesto), I want to share with you a selection of **disruptive points** that form my hypothesis as to why Governance thinking, especially in the Microsoft SharePoint world, is so utterly flawed, to the level that it brings tears to my eyes.

I know that there are a lot of you out there that really do get this concept of holistic Governance; but SharePoint is the fastest and largest grossing software platform in the world (Foley, 2011, http://bit.ly/SharePointMomentum), there are a huge number of you that aren't on the path to enlightenment.

It is you out there who are new to SharePoint, or are having Governance views forced upon you, or that are just plain confused that may be inadvertently preventing SharePoint implementations delivering real measurable business outcomes. I want to help you and your organisations get the true meaning of Governance, understand the implications of not getting it right and have a practical steer around implementing Governance today.

Let's be really clear, I know it's not really your fault that we are having so many Governance failures; we've all been brought up in analytic organisations.

What do I mean by analytic organisations? Well as Bob Marshall explains using his concept of 'Rightshifting' and the 'Marshall Model of Organisational Effectiveness' (Marshall, http://bit.ly/MarshallModel), analytic organisations are ones that typify, to a large extent, the principles of Scientific Management a.k.a. Taylorism. Typical characteristics of Analytical organisations include:

- A mechanistic view of organisational structure, e.g. functional silos and a focus on local optimisation
- Management tendency to focus on costs and efficiencies
- Middle-managers seen as owners of the way the work works, channelling organisational vision, allocating tasks and reporting on progress in a command and control style.

But enough words...

Let's get on the same page and create a shared understanding of the good, bad, ugly and damn right disruptive aspects of true SharePoint Governance.

What follows is my thesis; or to put it more accurately, this is the **Visual Thesis of Kubernáo**:

Thesis 1 - Be engulfed

Whatever you decide to do with your SharePoint Governance, don't do it by halves.

The value of Governance is in putting your heart and soul into the process.

Make sure your Governance touches every nook and cranny of your organisation, SharePoint platform and IT team.

Thesis 2 - Governance pirates

As mentioned previously:

- Everyone has a view to share
- Some people have tools
- A few of us have frameworks.

You need to make sure that whatever Governance approach you adopt, that it works for you and your organisation.

Don't be tricked out of your time and money.

Be sure of your goal and take what you need from the Governance pirates to achieve your goals.

Arrrrrr!

Thesis 3 - Bloody huge document

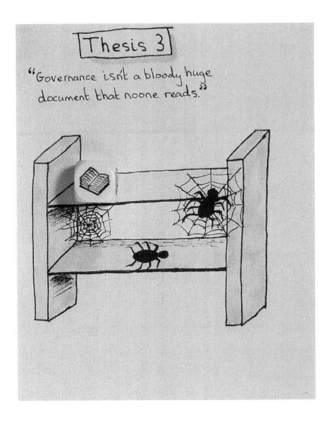

The size of your Governance document is completely irrelevant.

We'll discuss later in the book what Governance documents should contain, but let's cut out the crap that no-one is interested in.

Whatever you put in your Governance documents (first clue) make sure that they add value and people will actually want to read them, no point putting all your effort into something that will gather dust on shelves, physically or virtually!

Thesis 4 - Why?

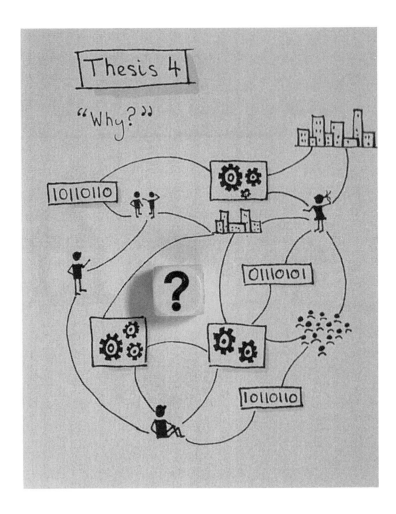

Whatever you're doing ask why?

- Ask why about the culture
- Ask why about the processes
- Ask why about the systems
- Ask why about the solution
- Ask why about the business
- Ask why about integrations
- Ask why about the requirements
- Ask why about the vision.

Then, make sure the Governance is the "How" to the "Why?" and that there's a shared understanding and commitment.

Thesis 5 - Banking crisis

The banks messed up, they caused a financial melt-down and we all suffered.

Perhaps a more appropriate application of Governance across the sector could have mitigated the chaos?

Let's not allow your project to mess up.

Let's not let allow your business users to suffer.

Take Governance seriously.

Take this book seriously.

Thesis 6 - Reflections

Your Governance should reflect your Vision.

Your SharePoint solution should reflect your Vision.

Hold up a magic mirror to your SharePoint solution and see what gets reflected.

How can you do this? Try this simple technique:

- **Step 1** - Project your SharePoint Intranet home page on a wall
- **Step 2** - Write the elements of your Vision onto a series of post-it notes
- **Step 3** - Put the post-it notes onto the projected image on the areas that may map
- **Step 4** - Evaluate the post-it notes left, why aren't these elements represented?

Vision, Governance and your solution should all be reflected in each other.

Thesis 7 & 8 - Visualise & socialise

Great Governance may as well be gathering dust on a shelf if no-one knows about it.

- Work out loud
- Evangelise your Governance
- Governance shouldn't just be in the heads and hard-drives of the IT department
- Governance shouldn't just be in documents
- Use visualisations to make Governance accessible
- Love your Governance
- Use different forms of communication to spread the message throughout the organisation
- Facilitate people sharing, discussing, evangelising and evolving your Governance
- Sketch your Governance
- Video and photograph your Governance
- Talk, shout or sing about your Governance
- Collaborate on your Governance
- Sell your Governance
- Be your Governance.

Get your Governance out there...

Thesis 9 - The black hole

Your SharePoint platform is going to slide into a very dark place without holistic Governance.

Be scared of the dark, bad things happen when the lights go out on your Governance.

View your Governance as a multitude of brightly lit torches, illuminating the way for your SharePoint solution.

Don't fall into the black hole!

Let this book be your guiding light, better still let this book be the spark that burns the old ways of Governance.

Thesis 10 - Certifiable

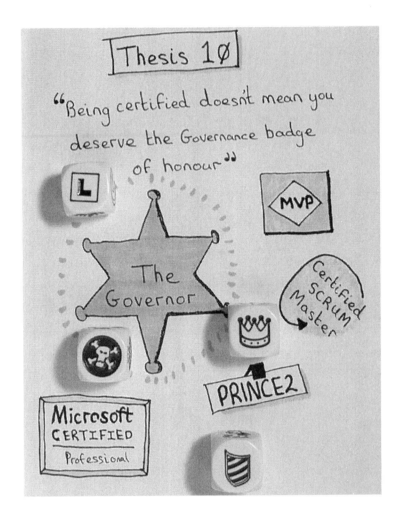

Whatever qualifications, certifications or level of standing within the community you have, please don't assume that you automatically get the Governance badge.

It's not something that's dished out readily.

Governance is very different from all those technical qualifications you may have or may be pursuing, like MCT, Scrum Master or Prince2.

They have a certain value, but not in the world of Governance.

The Governance badge of honour doesn't depend on technical prowess or nominations.

The Governance badge of honour comes from the realisation that:

- It is the business that leads the way for IT and SharePoint solutions.
- Complexity is what drives our direction of travel.
- A holistic approach will bring calm and business value to the SharePoint chaos that organisations are facing.

Governance is egalitarian! (http://bit.ly/Egalitarian)

Disruptive Governance
thinking for the masses

In at the deep end

The previous chapters have, I hope, given you an insight and perhaps even untapped your hidden passion for applying SharePoint Governance?

I appreciate that the rhetoric on its own is perhaps entertaining and insightful, but it doesn't give you, the reader of this Manifesto, a clear view about **how to progress**, except perhaps to focus significantly more time and effort on business and less focus on the IT aspects.

The remainder of this Manifesto is absolutely targeted at being the practical *'disruptive governance thinking for the masses'* that I promised you on the front cover.

Remember though, this is **not** your Grandma's (or your IT Team's) governance approach!

SharePoint Governance isn't a one-shot operation, you are going to make mistakes, I certainly did, and that's a key part of facilitating Governance in your organisation, you will I hope learn lots and it is going to be very messy at first, but it's the right thing to do, so let's go for it!

I've broken down my approach into what I refer to as **'The 7 Waves of SharePoint Governance'**. They are seven key areas of focus, that I recommend you and your organisation should adopt. It is a holistic approach, so you need to look at and take action in all 7 of the areas, in order to really deliver the true meaning of Governance and see the value of your SharePoint efforts.

But where the hell do you start?

Firstly, don't be afraid!

Let's remember back to a time when you were by the seaside and you put your toe in the cold ocean, it was freezing and unwelcoming and then someone pushes you in or you are just brave enough to dive in...

The icy water almost takes your breath away with the shock, but then you get used to the cold, when you are immersed by it and it doesn't feel quite as bad, perhaps it even feels comfortable!

This is what SharePoint Governance is like.

It can definitely be a scary, uncomfortable experience if you just play around the edges, but trust me if you dive in, be immersed in what you are doing, you'll see the value and it's context in your work and you will feel a whole lot better about the Governance challenges you are facing.

Secondly, please, please, **don't start with IT Governance**.

Governance should always be viewed from a business perspective, because that's where the difference we are trying to make is.

As we have seen earlier in my sailing analogy, just focussing on one or two areas can have some dire consequences, so focus holistically. I'll share the SharePoint Governance equivalents to you later in the Manifesto.

Focussing your Governance thinking and actions from a business perspective will keep you grounded with a more appropriate Governance world-view. For sure IT Assurance has to be a part of your Governance, so even with you focussing on a business point of view, I guarantee you won't forget the IT aspects, they will continue to happen with their own IT-led, good-practice momentum however much you ignore them!

Does size really matter?

One question that I am often asked, when talking to clients and consultants about Governance, is how do approaches differ depending on the size of organisation you are working with?

They ask,

> "...surely SharePoint Governance is different for a global organisation versus a medium sized company?"

My response is not what people are usually expecting.

Simplistically, when it comes to applying Governance in your organisation, Yoda sums it up best:

> "Do, or do not. There is no try." - Master Yoda

My approach to implementing SharePoint Governance **does not change** depending on size of organisation, SharePoint maturity, type of solution, business sector or any other facet.

We are either going to fully commit to investing time, money and effort into applying Governance, or we just walk away now and do the bare minimum IT focussed stuff that we did previously. The so called middle ground of 'try' is extremely counterproductive, but unfortunately it appears to be what happens in a huge number of organisations.

The reality is that the order, size and shape of your 'Governance Waves' does not matter, they will be unique to your organisation. This is the only real difference between applying Governance in different sized organisations. In fact this 'difference' is likely to be very much emergent. Your Governance is a continuous, infinite process influenced by business changes, maturity of the Governance already in place, the SharePoint functionality you continue to deploy, the business users and your experience and expertise.

I've worked with clients across a full range of Governance and SharePoint maturity. In each case we work together to assess where they are, their vision and then I look to positively disrupt their SharePoint Governance and work with them to deliver true organisational value from the platform.

Let me share with you my high-level Governance disruption plan:

- **Education** - Overview of the challenges, what Governance really is and the difference my approach can make
- **Vision** - Using *Collaborative Play* techniques we facilitate the customers vision for their SharePoint platform or project
- **Audit** - Using *Visual Templates* and *Collaborative Play* we facilitate what the organisation already has in place across the 7 waves
- **Action Plan** - Generation of a report summarising the previous activities and identifying the next steps.

This approach delivers immediate value in the form of the customers shared understanding of *'the difference SharePoint will make'* and how Governance can steer them towards that vision. From this solid base we can move forward and look in detail at how the 7 waves of SharePoint Governance can be uniquely applied in your organisation.

I'll go through in a little more detail how I approach this type of workshop engagement at the end of this section.

From this point onwards we have the boat really sailing in the right direction.

Why waves?

There are a number reasons why I use the term 'waves' in my governance approach analogy, here's just a small selection of them.

There are the obvious reasons such as my love for water and watching waves of absolutely any kind; I find them beautiful and infinitely interesting to watch, perhaps for me, almost hypnotic and very relaxing. I have also had the pleasure and pain of experiencing the power of waves whilst sailing, which makes me really appreciate their strength, awe and infinite variety.

There are also some less obvious, more theoretical reasons why it makes sense, at least to me, for Governance to be discussed in terms of waves.

For example, waves are created by the friction of wind against the water, similar perhaps to how Governance waves come about through the creative and organisational friction within a client's business.

Also, and this was a huge surprise to me:

Waves actually do not move forward.

Seriously, I'm not joking!

It is the energy within them that flows forward towards the shore, not the water itself.

Waves actually move in a kind of cyclic (continuous improvement?) manner, with water being sucked slightly towards the wave as the energy approaches, rising up, moving forwards slightly and either crashing in the surf or gently rolling back down to roughly its previous location.

Of course things like tide or currents do make water move or 'flow', but it's not the water in the wave itself... fascinating don't you think?

To find out more about waves of all kinds, you should definitely read *'The Wavewatchers Companion'* (Pretor-Pinney, 2011, http://bit.ly/WaveWatcher)

Summarising my obsession with waves and why we should picture our Governance activities as waves:

- Waves are unique
- Waves are a valuable energy resource
- Waves can be very disruptive
- Waves are one of the necessary artefacts of energy derived from the wind, earthquakes etc.
- Governance waves are the artefacts of the energy required to keep SharePoint moving towards its goal or vision.

As I said in an earlier section, your SharePoint Governance will be different from others, don't worry about it, there are some very good reasons for this and it doesn't mean that you are alone in your endeavours...

Surf's Up - Your Governance visualised

Picture this:

Your SharePoint team is the water

Your Organisation is the wind

Your SharePoint platform/project is the energy in the water

Your SharePoint Vision is a paradise island

The aim of the game is to make progress by transferring the energy (SharePoint) to the island (your vision)

Progress can be tracked by a cool surfboard or some random flotsam riding 'The 7 Waves of Governance'.

It should be clear from the analogy or personal experience, that there needs to be significant engagement and creative friction between the wind (your organisation) and the water (your SharePoint team) to generate the energy required to create the Governance waves we need to make progress towards our goal.

The effort (friction of wind against water) required to create the energy and hence the waves is directly proportional to what your vision is and how far away you are from it, so you really need to get a grip on these things, now!

So now we have identified some [Governance] waves, seven to be precise if we are to be effective. Now our goal in the SharePoint team (we will talk about the SharePoint team in more detail later in the book), is to help that energy (our SharePoint project / platform) travel from wherever we started, towards the vision as effectively as possible.

The progress (surfer or flotsam) is never going to be a straight-line, remember the water in each of the waves is moving in a circular motion around a *relatively* fixed point, so the surfer can 'ride each wave' until they're ready to move on...

That may be a weird explanation for something as dull as Governance, but this is what it looks like, in my mind, my whiteboard and occasionally on a client's wall:

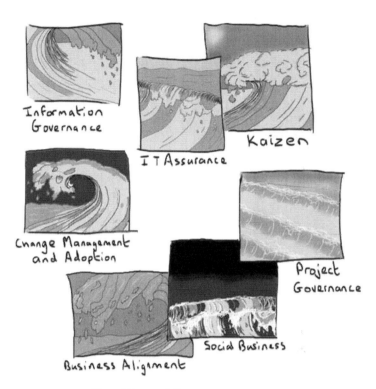

The 7 Waves of SharePoint Governance

Surfing the seven waves of Governance

As I have said previously, please don't make any assumptions or have any preconceptions about the importance, order or complexity of the 'waves', they all have an equal part to play as I will demonstrate later.

So what are the '7 Waves of SharePoint Governance'?

Simply put, Governance is all about putting 'things', not necessarily just large documents and strict rules, in place that help your project achieve its vision or goal.

We should consider that Governance is what helps you to ensure that the project or platform, in this case SharePoint, can deliver a positive difference to the business.

For most Governance initiatives and third-party tools, Governance starts and often finishes with IT and on rare occasions will also cover information management in some manner. In my opinion, as I hope I have articulated in the previous chapters, Governance is the basic success factors for your technology platform and therefore needs to be significantly more far reaching and cover much more ground than just technology in order to be successful.

My approach to Governance covers 7 specific areas (waves) and is defined as, in no particular order as:

- Business Alignment
- IT Assurance
- Project Governance
- Information Governance
- Change Management and Adoption
- Social Business
- Kaizen.

It is these areas that I focus all my governance thinking, workshops, documentation and on-going activities on.

Nothing is original

To be transparent, this model (The 7 Waves of SharePoint Governance) is an evolution of the work I did when I designed the *5 Pillars of SharePoint Governance* at 21apps a few years ago.

Through applying that original model across a number of clients and as an output of continuous improvement and further research into other models, I felt that my original work lacked some of the breadth and clarity that was needed to be truly successful in organisations. So over the last year, my thinking and the model have been evolved, clarified and extended to what you see before you on the pages of this Manifesto.

No doubt as I work with more organisations on their Governance challenges and I glean your feedback on the detail of the model within the following pages, the model will twist; morph and further value will emerge. That's the nature of Governance, which is why; although there is lots of rhetoric around, there are very few people or texts that really put a stake firmly into the ground.

I am sure that people will steal these governance ideas and make them their own, fit them around their technology platform or own world views, but that's fine after all as Austin Kleon says you should *"Steal like an artist"* (Kleon, 2012, http://bit.ly/StealItAll) and he highlights this great quote:

> *"Immature poets imitate; mature poets steal; bad poets deface what they take, and good poets make it into something better, or at least something different. The good poet welds his theft into a whole of feeling which is unique, utterly different from that from which it was torn; the bad poet throws it into something which has no cohesion."* - T.S. Eliot

I look forward to seeing what **you** create from this manifesto.

Share your results.

Showcase your remixes of this approach.

Shout about what works and what doesn't.

Your Governance should be collaborative, we can all help...

Please feel free to join "The SharePoint Governance Manifesto" public **LinkedIn group** (http://linkd.in/Y7zj9H) to carry on the conversations.

A final word of caution...

I use this approach all the time, what I'm imparting to you is my current perspective and articulation of what is, a very emergent practice.

If you're going to adopt this approach, then immerse yourself in it, as an appropriate level of Governance for your scenario is only achieved by applying effort in **all of these areas at the same time**, although reiterating what I mentioned earlier, the order and amount of effort each 'wave' requires will differ between organisations, platforms and projects.

What should also be noted about this approach to Governance is that not all areas rely on a check-list of activities or a tool to be delivered. Some of these areas require a change in behaviour, a change in focus or a mixture of activities in order to fully address the Governance pain-points.

What follows is a description of each of 'The 7 Waves of SharePoint Governance', the practicalities of implementing them and I high-light some of the repercussions of what happens if you skimp or ignore a wave, take heed! In each case I am consciously not covering everything about these areas, but what I am aiming to achieve is highlight the key game-changing ideas, concepts and techniques.

I hope that this approach and the level of detail I've gone to is enough to steer you onto a path of well governed SharePoint awesomeness!

Wave One - Business Alignment

Can you tell me how every feature you're deploying supports a real business goal?

No, then you must be working on an unimportant side-project...

SharePoint projects are people projects and people are a fundamental part of all organisations. People, as well as the businesses that employ them are complex, as we defined earlier in the book when I introduced the concept of the Cynefin Framework.

What is Business Alignment then?

Business alignment is about facilitating a change in the IT department and even organisational culture, to make a move towards aligning your projects, the technology platform and your business requirements to your organisational goals, not just focussing on individual, team or department needs. We must not forget that *everything* that we do in a SharePoint project has an impact on the end-users. Every action will create a change in behaviour or 'ways of working' for our users and conversely it will have a positive or negative effect on the overall organisation.

The pressure is on, we better get this bloody right!

This 'wave' has its roots in '**Systems Thinking**' and is very much a change in behaviours 'wave', seeking to move us from an analytic approach focussed on local optimisation, to a more whole-system view.

> *"Business and other human endeavours are also systems. They, too, are bound by invisible fabrics of interrelated actions, which often take years to fully play out their effects on each other. Since we are part of that lacework ourselves, it's doubly hard to see the*

whole pattern of change. Instead, we tend to focus on snapshots of isolated parts of the system, and wonder why our deepest problems never seem to get solved. Systems thinking is a conceptual framework, a body of knowledge and tools that has been developed over the past fifty years, to make the full patterns clearer, and to help us see how to change them effectively."
Peter Senge - The Fifth Discipline (Senge, 2006, http://bit.ly/SengeThinking)

The first step for us at a practical level is to make a move towards defining **measurable business outcomes** that facilitate progress towards your organisation vision and strategy. It is this shared understanding and commitment of the 'whole' that will help us govern effectively. Every activity we undertake within a SharePoint project and SharePoint business as usual, must be aligned to that organisation vision and strategy. We make positive steps towards being very clear as to what the real difference is that the technology, feature or process is going to make to our organisation.

Ask yourself the question:

> *"...is what we are doing adding measurable positive value to the organisation?"*

Your first response may well be 'what should I measure?' or 'how do I measure that fluffy stuff?' They are both very reasonable questions, but the answers are a huge topic in themselves.

I did attempt to answer this question from a SharePoint perspective, a couple of years ago, at a presentation I did at SharePoint Saturday UK 2011. I created a short eBook 'Measuring the Intangibles' to articulate these ideas, feel free to grab a copy here: http://bit.ly/MeasuringIntangibles.

As I mention in the eBook, currently my most significant influences in this field, come from the unlikely field of business models and start-ups.

I have long held the belief that [SharePoint] projects can be viewed through the lens of a business model. In fact I often use the concept of a *Business Model Canvas*, taken from the awesome book *Business Model Generation: A Handbook for Visionaries, Game Changers, and Challengers* (Osterwalder, Pigneur, 2010, http://bit.ly/SharePointBusinessModel) by the brilliant Alexander Osterwalder and Yves Pigneur. I've tweaked the canvas to be more SharePoint project aligned, but the fundamentals beautifully articulated in the book are bang on, I guess if you want more details about how I use this technique in projects, you'll have to get in touch, or maybe it will end up in my next book!

The other major influence in measuring SharePoint business value, is the work by Eric Ries on *The Lean Start-up*. His book, *The Lean Startup: How Constant Innovation Creates Radically Successful Businesses* (Ries, 2011, http://bit.ly/LeanSharePoint) contains some fantastic ideas that map really well onto measuring SharePoint value and are in synergy with working in a lean or agile way.

When you delve into the subject, depending on the scenario, there is a huge array of things that we can measure. Of course we need to remember to focus on measuring the *difference the project is going to make.* There will be the fairly obvious SharePoint related measures and progress towards business goals. But also consider, as myself and Andy Talbot (@SharePointAndy) recently discussed, the more qualitative measures that come from the field of community management.

As Andy rightly articulated:

> *"Don't focus on storage growth to measure success, but instead focus on community indicators, such as:"*

- Liveliness of pages

- Engagement of users across the organisation
- User Surveys
- Audit Results.

But back to the question in hand. If you cannot answer, honestly and positively, that your action, project or requirement is making a positive difference, then you should consider removing it from scope completely or perhaps spending some more time defining and aligning it.

This may seem a harsh decision to make, especially when you're on the receiving end, but waste is bad, local optimisation can be bad and we shouldn't fall into the trap of delivering SharePoint Celery for our clients. We need to ensure that the business and any associated processes, technology and cultural aspects are fully aligned. We need to have a clear, shared understanding and shared commitment for what the organisation and SharePoint are seeking to deliver and the difference we want to make.

Although not strictly within the remit of the book, I think it makes sense for me to impart a little knowledge and experience at this point, into how I help organisations achieve. Scratch that, how I help them start to make good progress towards business alignment, it's definitely a long journey!

All these techniques, derived from many sources, I term as 'collaborative play'.

This genre of facilitation techniques, which include Innovation Games, Gamestorming, Lego Serious Play etc. have the following traits:

- Collaborative
- Interactive
- Egalitarian
- Fun

- Creative
- Inclusive
- Disruptive
- and lots more!

There are a couple of specific techniques worth a mention, that I use to help my clients start to think more in terms of systems than local optimisation. What I don't usually do is deep dive into 'systems thinking' fundamentals, unfortunately most projects emerge from IT so full-scale organisational change is usually off-the cards, although a little 'skunkworks' (http://bit.ly/Skunkworks) organisational change, bottom-up never hurt, anyone did it?

Disruptive Tip No.1

Get a Vision

The first activity, **Cover Story** is taken from the book 'Gamestorming' (Gray, D., Brown, S., Macanufo, J., 2010,

http://bit.ly/GamestormingGovernance). It is a great collaborative exercise if facilitated well, for defining your SharePoint Vision, at a platform, project or even functional level.

Whatever the remit of an engagement, I always use this activity to ensure we all have a clear vision or goal to strive for during the engagement. As the activity is extremely collaborative, one advantage is that early on in the engagement I can gain an initial assessment of the dynamics of the stakeholders and whether they have a shared understanding of the goal. The activity also often unearths interesting insights into culture, personalities and the general dynamics of the group that I will need to work with and the organisation as a whole. In short, it can be a gold-mine of emergent value for you.

The exercise asks the participants to imagine that the project/initiative that they are working on has been successfully completed, actually it has not just been successful, but earth shatteringly awesomely successful! So much so that an international trade publication or Time magazine, have decided to run a full front-cover story on the project and the difference it made to the organisation and its customers!

On a whiteboard or very large piece of paper, in groups of 4-8, depending on the number of stakeholders, the participants build out the template I've sketched below using sketches, words, craft materials or post-it notes:

Gamestorming 'Cover Story'

The areas on the visual canvas are used to help derive certain 'vision' details and are defined as follows:

- **Cover** - This is the front-cover and should contain the bold, hard-hitting story and perhaps images, that articulate the big story and the high-level difference that you have made
- **Big Headlines** - Here you convey the substance of the story, more detail, but still hard-hitting and usually aspirational
- **Brainstorm** - This area is used for 'storing' any ideas that don't fit anywhere else, but quite often contains very interesting insights
- **Images** - I tend not to use this for SharePoint Governance work, but the areas is meant for any visuals that help define your vision and the difference this has made
- **Quotes** - This is really useful, what would people say about this great success? What do project members, business users, stakeholder or even customers say about what's been delivered and the difference it has made?
- **Side-Bar** - This area is for capturing the details; I encourage participants to use this area to come up with measures for the difference they have made articulated in %'s, $'s, £'s, time etc.

The resulting visual canvas is both beautiful, insightful and a clear message, in the words of business stakeholders, of what they are trying to achieve. What you will also find is that as the group or spokesperson report back their 'cover story', they will be **telling you a story**. Actively listen and make copious notes, because as all great facilitators know, there is substantial value in what they say as well as what they have created.

For a Governance project this vision is **invaluable** as you can and will, continually refer back to it, as you steer your SharePoint project or platform towards its goal.

In my experience it's what can make the difference between technology mayhem and SharePoint sanity!

Disruptive Tip No.2

Goal Align EVERYTHING!

Another tip I'd like to impart is much simpler, but equally effective and disruptive in a range of scenarios. It's all about **Goal Alignment** and it is a simple means of sense-checking what's going on in a project:

> *Ensuring that we are not delivering the wrong things really effectively!*

In my eyes, in order to truly reach the karmic state of delivering maximum business value, everything that happens in your technology platform and any subsequent projects **must be aligned** to directly or indirectly making a positive difference to your organisation. If it isn't then don't do it, or re-define it. Agile and lean approaches to manufacturing, technology and business, all strive to reduce waste, and however you're implementing your SharePoint solutions, I think you should to. It may seem harsh or even verging on heretical to go around your projects telling people to stop what they are doing and move onto something else, but consider these common SharePoint 'feature requests':

- Move the 'Search' box to the left-hand side of the screen
- Animate the menu structure
- Make SharePoint more 'Social'
- Have an IA based on our ever-changing organisational structure
- Make the text flash if it's important.

Seriously, do any of these actually add any value to your solution or to the business? The likely answer in all the cases above is no they don't, so let's stamp out this waste and focus on delivering the right things really well.

Now I am not saying that we shouldn't have solutions that look good and exude a great user experience; but let's focus our precious resources on the things that really matter first.

This approach, albeit perhaps very annoying to the recipient, is relevant whatever phase or activity you are doing whether it's coding a custom web-part, branding, creating a custom list, facilitating requirements, delivering training or managing on-going change.

How do we achieve this project nirvana of just doing the things that matter and make a positive difference?

The answer is 'Goal Alignment'.

Why? Fundamentally, this is a very effective approach to ensuring a shared understanding and allows you to question the value of what you are doing. If you already have a vision, then this is a simple validation technique:

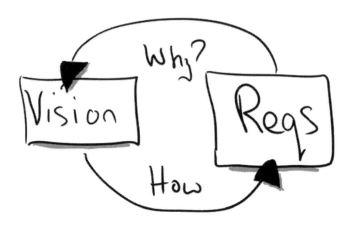

Goal Alignment Cycle

For every programme, project, requirement or technical feature we can ask 'why' it supports the Vision, if it does, great; but if it doesn't then we either need to redefine it or remove it from scope, as it must be waste, for this project at least.

This is a typical line of 'enquiry' or 'why validation':

> **Technical feature** *'supports a'* **Business Requirement** *'which delivers value for a'* **Project** *'which enables business outcomes within a'* **Programme** *'that supports a'* **Vision** *'that is in line with the'* **Organisational Strategy**.

Working in the opposite direction, you are validating 'how' things will be implemented and is in my experience, very useful for ensuring that requirements are fully covered by your technical solution.

'Business Alignment' is therefore a key concept that keeps our SharePoint platform sailing towards our goal, whatever changes occur around us.

But what if we don't pursue Business Alignment?

Basically you will have a failing project or an inadequate platform or just a set of waste features. What you will have delivered will be a pure technology project, it will be SharePoint Celery, nothing more.

Without business alignment, I would wager good money that what you are working on, will achieve a negative ROI and you will have been spending time on requirements, activities or even whole projects that really aren't adding much value at all. In extreme cases and these aren't as rare as you would wish, you may even be counterproductive in the overall business scheme of things.

That certainly isn't cool!

That isn't what you're being paid to do.

The problems don't just stop with a few wasted opportunities for value.

Nope, once you let this cat out of the bag you'll find yourself being blindly led down the wrong path...

There will be enhancements, bugs and changes being demanded by the business to the features and projects they don't need and then what about the future re-branding project or the upgrade project?

Think about all that extra work you need to do to style and brand features no one wants, think of the additional complexity and risk to your upgrade projects because of features and requirements that no one will use or gain value from? Let's face it this is not a situation that any of us really want.

I hope this serves as a clear wake-up call that not having business alignment can seriously screw-up projects, your career and the IT departments reputation. All for the sake of not having a shared understanding/commitment to the vision, amplified by not using goal alignment to maintain a steady course.

Wave Two - IT Assurance

Wave Three - Project Governance

Look deep inside your current project and tell me this.

Is your project approach and processes hindering the delivery of real business value?

Perhaps a more familiar topic to you is Project Governance?

"...Hey Ant aren't we doing this well already?

Well maybe, maybe not.

Within the context of the '7 waves', Project Governance is focused on ensuring that we utilise an appropriate project methodology, for what we are implementing. Ideally in my experience this should be an agile approach (Scrum, Lean, Kanban etc.). We also need to ensure that both the project and all its underlying tasks, are aligned to the business vision we have collaboratively defined for the project and the organisations overall strategy. This goal alignment, as we have already discussed, is critical for the delivery of a successful project.

Whatever project approach you adopt, it is key to ensure that the project and its stakeholders have a shared understanding and shared commitment to delivering both the technology and change management aspects of the project and that they are aligned with the Project Vision and organisational goals.

This is one of the key drivers that influenced my move from analytical tools and techniques to facilitation and collaborative play (Innovation Games, Gamestorming and sketching). Remember the 'Death of BA' I wrote about earlier in the Manifesto? Projects that utilise collaboration technology need to be approached in a different way. They need to be well aligned to the business, have transparency and make a difference to the organisation.

I'm not going to talk much about Project Governance, because the reality is there is a heap of content and approaches already out there...also, I'm not a qualified Project Manager or scrum master! What I will state, very clearly and confidently is the following:

- Don't be half-baked, choose a project approach and do it properly; taking the best-bits from methodologies usually equals catastrophic failure
- If you're doing collaboration, social or people-based projects then use an agile approach
- Don't question the previous two points, just do it!
- Make sure that everything in the project is business aligned
- Start small and work towards delivering a continuous stream of measurable business outcomes
- Remember that swimming against a waterfall is knackering and ends in disaster!
- Projects aren't about managing tasks and stakeholders, they're about delivering value.

But are projects just about plans, kanban boards, sprints, flow, stand-ups, post-it notes and meetings?

Nope... What else do you think they are about?

People, team members, users and project resources perhaps? This is an area of Project Governance that I do think is often missed or under represented.

I suggest we consider at this point your actual SharePoint project delivery team. Just because your project, requirements and stakeholders are all aligned correctly, doesn't necessarily mean that your project team are.

Think about it a moment, nope longer, a little longer.... That's about enough time.

It makes absolute sense, based on my experiences, working with a plethora of different teams, for you to ensure that the shared understanding and shared commitment extends through to your project delivery and support teams. The reality is that no matter how well everything else is aligned, if your SharePoint team (internal, external, outsourced, contracted etc.) aren't properly aligned then your project will come unstuck, very quickly.

One great way we have found in facilitating and aligned delivery and support team is to create a SharePoint Centre of Excellence (CoE) within your organisation and I'll talk more about that in a later section of the book.

What will happen if we don't have any specific focus on Project Governance?

There are three intertwined impact zones, both equally painful, if we don't pay enough focus to doing Project Governance properly:

- Project delivery **effectiveness**
- Project, stakeholder and user **happiness**
- Business **value**.

Not focussing adequately on Project Governance and business alignment in all project activities, results in project team confusion, mixed priorities, a lack of shared understanding and shared commitment. You will also find, and I bet a lot of you have experienced this first hand, that without an appropriate project approach and alignment, there is no way that you can effectively measure progress against our goals. Sure the tasks on the project plan may be 80% complete, but how does that equate to progress delivering value, supporting a vision? How long will that last 20% take? Exactly!

Happiness...

Is that really an impact?

I sincerely think it is. Grumpy stakeholders, fed up architects, disillusioned developers, un-loved support guys, unhappy users...

All of these will have a negative impact on productivity, business value, stakeholder engagement and ultimately the sustainability of your SharePoint platform.

You need to work towards seeing happy smiling faces in your projects and when you talk to the business about SharePoint you shouldn't be greeted by groans, shudders and sobbing.

We've already talked extensively about change in SharePoint projects and the business world. However it's worth reiterating, because as things change within the context of our projects, such as requirements, financial constraints, time constraints, vision and stakeholders; they can have a devastating effect on a project.

How the hell do you cope with a constantly changing project plan, evolving assumptions and stakeholder expectations, if you don't have the ability to work with them, bend, flex and be steered appropriately?

As I mentioned earlier the Project Manager's role (and that of the delivery team) is not about the administration of a plan, it's got to be all about delivering value. The plan is just a communications tool about maintaining a shared understanding and expectation, so let's use new, innovative, non-IT approaches, tools and techniques that will enable and facilitate this.

A last point, which I added more as some food for thought, during the review process, a few months after this section was originally written.

> *"Don't view Project Governance as a Gantt chart or a kanban board, think back to the Pyramids, Stonehenge, the first organisation or the first building... None of them had access to MS Project."*

This thought is reinforced by something I read in 'Social Business By Design: Transformative Social Media Strategies for the Connected Company' (Hinchcliffe, D., Kim, P., 2012, http://bit.ly/SocialByDesign)

> *"Following a plan is increasingly less important than responding actively and effectively to change."*

My take on this great quote, is that we should all be creating change, not mindlessly following and maintaining a sterile plan...

Wave Four - Information Governance

After people, information is your organisations most important asset.

Is your SharePoint platform loving or hurting this precious resource?

I see Information Governance as a game of two halves.

Information is a core aspect for most organisations and therefore 99% of organisations (made up statistic) rely on information, data, processes, records, knowledge, experience and expertise for the successful use, adoption and on-going business value of their Share-Point platform.

Most of this 'information' is created, consumed and driven by individuals in your organisation and external partners and it is this collective intelligence that enables our businesses to prosper, innovate and achieve their organisational vision and strategy. Information, be it in the form of content, documents, images, videos, records or social interactions and connections needs to be facilitated, managed and governed in order to deliver true value to an organisation.

Information Governance in the context of the '7 Waves of Share-Point Governance' touches the whole of the organisation. It is the wide scope of activities that ensures that any content you have, in whatever form it may take, is capable of adding value to the organisation and supporting the vision and expected business outcomes.

Information Governance is very much a joint responsibility between the business users and the SharePoint Centre of Excellence or project team.

Information Governance encompasses both Information Architecture (IA) and Information Management (IM):

- **Information Architecture** - Metadata, taxonomy etc.
- **Information Management** - Process, workflow, security etc.

It is this combination of approaches that can, if applied appropriately, help to facilitate alignment of all the information that is in, or impacted by your solution to your business goals.

Many of you will I am sure, have some level of Information Governance in place, shame on you if you don't; maybe around records management or SharePoint site creation or perhaps document security. But are you continually reviewing this Governance? Are you ensuring that how SharePoint stores, manages and presents your organisations information fully supports the organisations on-going information needs in line with the Project Vision and organisational goals?

Information Governance differs greatly depending on the type of solution you are implementing and the type of organisation and sector you are operating in. Despite this, there are a number of Governance actions we can all take into account, in any SharePoint implementation.

Information Architecture is predominantly focussed on helping your organisation *use* your solution. Findability, putability, navigation, audience targeting and context are the key facets of this area. From a Governance perspective, we are only really looking to ensure that the solution makes sense to the end user and that we provide active support for the user and the solution to deliver business value.

What should you include in your Information Architecture activities? Well this isn't an all-inclusive list, but in my experience these are the key elements:

- Site structure
- Navigation methods

- Metadata
- Folksonomy
- Search
- Context
- Content types.

I've witnessed a number of examples across public and private sectors, where Information Architecture is over complicated and becomes a huge stumbling block, both conceptually and technically for projects. In fact this has for some, become such a problem that it has shrouded SharePoint as a platform in a cloud of negativity that it really doesn't deserve.

As an example, a few years ago I was involved in engaging a public sector organisation in implementing an organisation wide information management solution. Despite the technology and the implementation team being more than capable to deliver, the project stalled significantly. Why? Because at a conceptual level the information managers and business stakeholders across the business couldn't agree on what metadata they should use! This stumbling block prevented the project delivering value because it was adding complexity and they weren't thinking about Governance in terms of steering and value.

Some of the key themes I convey to my clients around how to pragmatically approach the Information Architecture aspects of Governance include:

- Keep it simple
- Make sure all your IA activities align with the vision
- Drive your IA from your vision and the measurable business outcomes, anything else is just waste
- Implement a base IA that supports your vision and requirements

- Use Kaizen (Continuous Improvement) and emergent functionality such as open term sets and Enterprise Keywords (folksonomy), in order to evolve and expand your IA.

A lightweight technique I regularly adopt, is to facilitate an IA workshop session. This allows participants to visually map IA elements (metadata, navigation etc.) to the high-level screen design and functionality. This gives us the opportunity to collaboratively look at what the minimum Information Architecture elements are, that will support the functionality they require and aligns to the vision. Progressing screen by screen, this is a collaborative and open activity, allowing me to validate peoples thinking and alignment to deliver the most pragmatic and vision aligned IA that we can.

On this subject, I'm often surprised as to how few organisations think about implementing contextual features in their intranets and knowledge management solutions. For me this is one of the great aspects of SharePoint that can, when used appropriately deliver significant value. For those on SharePoint 2013, with more and more functionality driven by search and metadata this is a no brainer surely?

For those that don't know what I'm talking about, I'm just referring to the practice of making visible, relevant or contextual content from elsewhere in your solution (or organisation) and presenting it 'alongside' the information, page, data that your user is looking at. Think of it as value-add info driven by metadata.

Remember:

Governance is about steering.

We should only be looking to implement just enough information architecture, just in time...

Information Management is one of those areas that is, in the old analytic SharePoint world, the most well represented, albeit quite often not appropriately. This aspect of Information Governance concerns itself with information processes, workflow, security and the like. It is the rules that need to be applied to ensure that information is used appropriately and users stay 'safe' within the solution.

Think of Information Management as the laws or a leash for users. We want our SharePoint solution to deliver value, help the business achieve its vision and for the users to maximise their appropriate use of the platform.

What we really don't want is users getting in trouble, inefficiencies, law breaking, distrust, being sued, getting things wrong, unhappiness, going out of business, being blamed or anything else bad.

In order to do avoid the negativity, I think Information Management needs to follow these straightforward tenets:

- Compliance, rules, law and legislation are boring but very necessary - **Keep your users out of trouble!**
- Users are the key to business value, not the IT department - **Give the business enough freedom to innovate**
- We don't know what the future of the platform or the business may hold - **Allow and facilitate emergent behaviours and value**
- SharePoint projects are people projects - **Support the different ways of working that exist in your organisation.**

I'm not going to apologise for what I am about to say, yes I am repeating myself, but most of what I'm thinking, writing and saying needs repeating continually.

Remember, Governance is about steering, we should only be looking to implement just enough information management, just in time...

What if we don't apply Information Governance?

Your SharePoint platform will go pear-shaped (that's not a good shape by the way)...

It may not happen like the big bang of not enough disk space or a mis-specified server farm, but gradually over time the problems will emerge, with ever increasing impact until your organisation refers to your SharePoint platform as a crock of s*!t.

Some of the major impacts of this will likely include some or all of the following and more. Employees won't be able to find what they're looking for (information, data, knowledge etc.), you won't deliver your anticipated business outcomes, you'll have disgruntled business users and the absolute killer... people will revert back to using email!

> *"The greatest challenge has to do with making technologists sufficiently user-like. Getting them to stop thinking in terms of bells and whistles and elaborate functionality, and to start thinking instead about busy users with short attention spans who need to get something done, and who can always reach for email."* - Andrew Macafee

Whatever the impact, it certainly won't be pretty and will most definitely contribute to the SharePoint Celery Effect we discussed earlier in the book.

Information and the way that people in your organisations and systems interact with it, is at the heart of your SharePoint platform, don't let them down, make it work for them!

Information Governance, looking at your solution from a day-to-day use perspective, is *one of the most important* aspects of Governance for the end-user.

However you achieve it, you should strive to educate the end user community (maybe consider using Tummelers or community managers), as to why it is so important that they take Information Governance and its SharePoint idiosyncrasies seriously.

Explain why we are using metadata, adding terms to folksonomies and creating content types, what is the value to them, their teams and the organisation as a whole. We need to start to make the change to an organisational culture that takes a more mature approach to knowledge work. We should reinforce the fact that when each individual user is applying metadata, adding terms, using content types, commenting and rating, that they are adding to the overall awesomeness of the SharePoint solution.

We are back to the old adage of:

"Garbage in, Garbage out."

We need to break this cycle of crap going into our information systems and become exemplars of the knowledge economy!

Wave Five - Change Management & Adoption

Technology is stupid, but the people in your organisation aren't.

Give them the respect and support they deserve, to do their jobs and help the organisation achieve its vision.

When I talk to clients about SharePoint Governance, the concept of 'to steer' and some of the other topics we've covered and then I start to tell stories about Change Management and User Adoption, the typical emotional response, I can see it in their eyes...

"...what the hell do any of these things have to do with Governance... He's gone too far now!"

Is this a step too far?

Is this hitting the hammer way too hard, when I'm putting a stake in the ground for the definition and approach to a better way to do SharePoint Governance?

In my experience and opinion it isn't, in fact this area seems to get seriously short-changed under normal circumstances, so including it here and in your Governance plans, at least gives us a chance to redress some of the balance in an explicit manner.

Back to basics, why do I include Change Management and Adoption in this Governance approach?

Firstly, let's define in broad terms what I mean:

This area of Governance refers to all the activities and initiatives required to embed change and enable technical solutions to be appropriately adopted within an organisation. This is so **much more** than simple training and nominating some unengaged, confused, reluctant change champions. This is about implementing an aligned change programme, taking user adoption seriously and even going as far as considering community management and other initiatives that will, all together, support and amplify the changes in behaviour, ways of working and business outcomes that we require in order to meet our vision.

Secondly, if we are going to be steering towards a business focussed vision, then we better involve and engage with the business. All businesses rely on its people and if those people aren't engaged then they'll do their damn best to steer us away from our vision. So considering these facts, this is why Change Management and User Adoption is so fundamentally critical in ensuring we don't deliver SharePoint Celery and we do steer a SharePoint path towards the business vision in a sustainable and appropriate manner.

Putting it simply, without the support of 'people' SharePoint isn't going anywhere fast. From a sailing perspective this means your boat will be head to wind or worse still, sunk...

So what do we need to do, in order to deliver an appropriate level of Change Management and User Adoption within our SharePoint Governance?

The full answer is a huge topic, way too complex and detailed for these pages. What I want to cover in this manifesto, are just enough insights to take your minds above and beyond the boring and relatively ineffective 'train the trainer' or 'branded mouse mat' approaches. I'm hoping to disrupt your current world views on this topic and get you thinking in a new, more effective and value driven way.

Let's start with quite a flippant statement, but one that we shouldn't ever lose sight of:

SharePoint is just a set of web pages.

How hard is it really?

Now I agree the reality is that within those web pages there is much complexity, but we really shouldn't forget that this is not balancing on a trapeze wire over the Grand Canyon or sailing around the world or building a space rocket, within the context of SharePoint we are *just* clicking on links, reading things, typing stuff in boxes, attaching things etc. it's when we let things get complex that we run the risk of capsizing SharePoint.

We've also talked at length about having a clear Vision for the difference that SharePoint should make to your organisation and your stakeholders. My experience is that your users will either have a shared understanding and commitment to this or not and we can categorise individuals into three distinct camps.

If they 'get it' then they are awesome and an asset to your Share-Point platform, maybe these people could be your SharePoint Tummelers? (more on Tummelers later)

If they don't 'get it' then they're not likely to be using SharePoint at all; this is a pain, not a great situation, but I suggest you leave these people well alone and let the HR and Personal Development Reviews sort them out, because if SharePoint is a strategic platform in your organisation, eventually it will bite the non-believers in the arse.

The most challenging and dangerous camp of people in your organisation though, are the ones that kind of get it. They use SharePoint, but not for the right reasons, they're not striving for the same vision as you and they are out in the business muddying the waters for the other users. These people need taking by the hand and educating ASAP into the right frame of mind. The problem with these confused individuals is that their behaviours and the messages they send out to their friends and colleagues are inconsistent. They send links to documents because it's 'easier', even though they know that's not the right thing to do, they keep local copies of documents 'just in case' and they only use SharePoint when there really isn't any other viable option (remember Andrew MacAfee's quote earlier in the Manifesto - email is likely to always be a viable option!).

But the real problem with this group of SharePoint [partial] users is that they are often in senior positions, with significant influence on the rest of your user base!

In terms of our wave analogy, these people act like a layer of oil on the water, preventing waves from forming and stopping the energy flow towards the beach.

One of the biggest hurdles for end users and SharePoint solutions, is that they are not connected to their *flow of work* and they don't see the context or 'difference it will make'.

This is why SharePoint Change Management and User Adoption are so important, but also so very complex.

Everyone works differently!

The best you can do is to make sure that you have a clear vision, as we discussed previously and facilitate business requirements that are articulated in terms of the business (not technical features), aligned to the vision and measurable through the difference they will make.

So how can you and your organisation start to think in terms of 'why?' or the difference something will make? Well Simon Sinek articulates this much better than I can and I would recommend at a minimum you stop reading, invest 18 minutes and go watch the TED video of his talk 'How great leaders inspire action' recorded at TEDxPuget Sound (Sinek, 2009. http://bit.ly/Sinek-why).

Did you enjoy it? I thought so.

His book 'Start With Why' is awesome too (Sinek, 2011, http://bit.ly/Sinek-Why-Book).

So what does 'Start With Why' really mean in the context of your SharePoint projects?

> *"People don't buy what you do, they buy why you do it."* - Simon Sinek

The key part of that quote is *'Why we do it'*...

Hmmm, why are you doing SharePoint?

Cool technology, the CIO said so, our competitors are doing it, or my all-time favourite:

> *"..Microsoft said that a bicycle shop saved millions of cash implementing SharePoint..!"*

Crap reasons I hope you agree?

If we all agree that SharePoint projects are people projects, do we really think that our business users are going to find these compelling reasons to use SharePoint? Nope, we need deeper, more business aligned reasons and that's where Simon Sinek comes in.

Simon says...

OK let's not get into that game, but we do need to change our mindset and SharePoint project delivery, approach from being subservient, doing as we are told, implement the technology just because we can, to a grown up approach of focussed on 'why'.

If we only ever undertake SharePoint activities that facilitate or directly make a positive difference to our business, that puts us in a great place. If we can articulate and measure how our SharePoint activities help the organisation achieve its vision, then we will make a real business difference.

If we do all these things, then our customer, the business user, will be using SharePoint because they really get it, they grok (it means to **really** understand and is a very cool word to use) the why, they are engaged and positive change *will* happen.

The way I try to make sense of this, is to pretty much always run a 'vision' session at the start of an engagement or project with my clients. There are two key benefits for doing this - Firstly it really helps me understand the organisational dynamics and rationale behind what they are doing, the SharePoint project.

Secondly and arguably more importantly, is that for most organisations, they are focussed on the technology or pseudo-business requirements that they think are business led. This exercise gives me the opportunity to proactively reveal the error of their ways and start to change the SharePoint stakeholders thinking, certainly in terms of SharePoint, but ideally more generally at a business level.

I hope that makes sense to you? I truly do believe that the path to SharePoint success and great Governance is by understanding the difference you are making and why you're doing it.

The last thing to consider in a little detail, is the over-hyped and very misunderstood term of *Gamification*. You may or may not be particularly aware of the concept and the reality is that SharePoint as a platform and even the offerings of its vendors, don't really offer that much in the way of Gamification features. There are a few offerings if you look hard enough and I expect this market to blossom over the next two years.

Formally, Gamification is defined as:

> *"the use of game-thinking and game mechanics in non-game contexts in order to engage users and solve problems."*

But most people think that Gamification just means rewards, badges and leaderboards, such as those found in Foursquare or Runkeeper and other social applications.

The reality is that those concepts only exist in those applications in order to **motivate** us. The writers of those solutions, just like game designers, are using Gamification techniques to reinforce and encourage the behaviours that are going to be of value to them, they use them to encourage participation and to help steer people towards a goal, whatever that may be.

So do we think implementing game thinking and mechanics into SharePoint such as rewards, badges and leader boards is going to be of value to our Governance quest and help us in our Change Management and Adoption activities?

The answer, like so many other things with SharePoint, is that it depends.

The introduction of Gamification into your SharePoint solution needs careful consideration, done right and you will win big time, done for the wrong or no reason, then you will have a costly failure.

If you just implement an ad-hoc combination of rewards, badges and leader boards or any other game mechanic, without any fore-thought the likelihood is you will fail on your quest and there is evidence that you will in fact negatively impact user adoption.

But if you think carefully about the changes in behaviour that you are trying to facilitate and have a vision, then Gamification can be an extremely powerful tool. In corporate scenarios, badges aren't likely to be a great motivator, leader boards can have a negative effect, especially when done on an organisational level, but if you look at your organisational culture, the behaviours you're trying to change or reinforce and the vision you are looking to achieve, then you will be able to identify ways in which game-mechanics can be used to positively influence both change management and on-going user adoption.

Some examples I have seen work include:

- **Rewards** such as training vouchers, flexi-time additions, allocated parking spaces etc.
- **Input** into personal development reviews, influencing promotion and opening up career opportunities etc.
- **Badges** and awards indicating achievements such as SME level 2, Tummeler, Tagging Master, Knowledge Ninja, Top Content Rater, Social Butterfly etc.

What is very true though, is that this area requires significant investment from a technology perspective, to implement, from a conceptual perspective to ensure that the game mechanics support what you are trying to achieve and above everything else, is very much dependent on your organisational culture.

Finally for now, I want to introduce two pivotal concepts that I apply within Change Management and User Adoption Governance. These two concepts I am passionate about and feel are fundamental to the success and sustainability of your SharePoint Governance.

They are the creation of what I term the *SharePoint Centre of Excellence* or *SharePoint Guild* within your organisation, this coupled with another (slightly strangely named) concept called *SharePoint Tummelers.*

These will become your most potent tonic for SharePoint success if approached correctly. Both of these concepts will be subject to much greater explanation later in the Manifesto.

What if we don't apply Change Management and Adoption?

In the context of technology solutions that address business, social and collaborative challenges people often say "Build it and they will come".

"No they bloody won't!"

Is always my response!

If we ignore Change Management and Adoption in our on-going governance planning and execution then the result is pretty simple, things will fail.

It may not be SharePoint Celery that we end up with, but the effect is very similar, we certainly won't be able to deliver on our vision, adoption of the solution will dwindle rapidly and any hope of and changing behaviours within the organisation won't even get off the ground.

From past experience, there is every likelihood that your organisation and the SharePoint platform will end up in a worse place if this area of governance isn't taken seriously.

Remember, if people aren't using the solution, it really doesn't matter how well all the other waves of Governance are covered, you're going to be playing the blame game and looking for a new career and there's no a badge or leader board for that!

Wave Six - Social Business

Does your organisation still want to be in business at the end of this decade?

Then don't ignore 'social' or it'll bite you in the arse.

This is another area where I often catch my clients looking at me cautiously, perhaps wondering if I'm going to get them to **'Poke'** or **'Like'** their Governance!

You'd think I'd have learnt by now and started playing a little safe with my Governance thinking, but the reality is that including 'social business' within your Governance is becoming ever more important. Whatever the focus of your project, implementing it on a social or collaborative platform is going to change the way people work in your organisation.

The majority of organisations that we as 'SharePoint-ers' get involved with, are focussed predominantly on knowledge work. These people now work in a much more open and social way, not a mechanistic process driven one, therefore we need to consider social interactions, culture, complexity theory, systems thinking, organisational change and new ways of working, throughout the platforms lifetime.

Dion Hinchcliffe et al in *'Social Business By Design'* describe Social Business as:

> *"the intentional use of social media to drive meaningful, strategic business outcomes"*

Howards Schultz, CEO of Starbucks, discusses in 'Onwards: How Starbucks Fought For Its Life without Losing Its Soul' (Schultz, H, 2011, http://bit.ly/SavingStarbucksSoul) how 'social features' and working more openly enabled what is called 'creative tension':

"Over the years, our forums have yielded creative tension and critical feedback, which is good for the organization."

So working as a Social Business and governing this aspect appropriately, is not just about turning on the social features in your SharePoint farm, although that is certainly one aspect, it is more about culture, your businesses operating model and the very essence of how most organisations will need to do business in the future.

Although I have great aspirations for organisations in this area of Governance, for the most part, I have found that exploring this area of Governance with my clients, has tended to be more of a **wake-up call for the business**, rather than an exercise in refining Governance practices.

Although this is a disappointing lack of traction for the moment, progress is being made and at the time of writing, being a social business tends to be the realm of the early adopters so it's not at all surprising.

I see this as a fantastic opportunity for organisations to begin to **future-proof their SharePoint Governance** approach and a way to kick-start them into looking at how their operating model is changing, with regards to working and doing business in a more social manner.

Experience is showing that the outputs in this area of Governance so far, have tended to be focussed on engaging with the Executive team to ascertain their take on 'social business' and then assessing the impacts that this will undoubtedly have on internal systems such as SharePoint, general working practices and of course organisational culture.

That said, my hope and expectation over the coming year or so, is that Social Business will become more of a fundamental part of Governance thinking and organisations business as usual.

But my organisation is unsocial and so am I!

This isn't a surprise, as mentioned in the previous paragraphs, you are not alone so do not despair... but do take action, today!

The truth is if you leave 'Social Business' out of your Governance plans, then the impact for most organisations will be minimal at most over the next year or so. But if you don't start thinking about 'Social Business' now, the impacts may well be significant in the future.

We all know that we have a new generation of knowledge workers entering the field of influence for our SharePoint projects, that have been brought up in the midst of a 'social revolution'. The future impact on our platforms, projects, ways of working and business visions is going to be hugely significant.

Think for a moment about the impact on your SharePoint project if you were delivering a solution for 'digital natives' like your kids or nieces and nephews? They have much higher expectations on technology and social engagement than we ever had. Ask yourself this question:

> *How would I approach SharePoint and its Governance if I was delivering a solution for the kids of today?"*

That's a scary question isn't it?

'Social Business' Governance requires attention, engagement and action from a technology, culture and business perspective. If you don't start to look at these areas now, then over the coming year you will find very quickly, that SharePoint adoption will be negatively impacted, solutions will not be able to adapt to the changing workforce, evolving working patterns and business changes and ultimately the solution will not deliver it's true potential over the long term.

Implementing 'Social Business' Governance is a long-game, which needed starting yesterday.

Let's close this section on a more hopeful note. There are some organisations that did start *yesterday.* Perhaps with very tentative steps, but there are examples out there, of organisations starting to embrace social business and looking at how these concepts can be embedded in their SharePoint solutions.

I've worked with a global brewery using Yammer to explore emergent knowledge management, get a feeling for community management, break down organisational hierarchies and exploring how they can integrate this into SharePoint.

I've consulted with clients who are leveraging their external social media approaches and guidelines to influence how they work in a more social way internally.

Third-party vendors are pushing the boundaries with social add-ons, innovation management and gamification features.

So you see, the move has already started and it's not just with Microsoft adding a few more social features to the platform, it's starting with people and culture and ways of working.

Remember, it's **you** that needs to make that first 'social business' step.

Start by talking and influencing stakeholders, not by installing technology stuff.

Wave Seven - Kaizen

Are you looking forward to spending the next 6 months delivering a SharePoint solution that no one wants and very few people will use?

There is a huge amount of texts, thinking, approaches and academic evidence around the benefits of Kaizen. I recommend that you dive in and get reading!

SharePoint Governance should be regarded as being an infinite cycle of activities and engagement with the business. For this reason the reality of the '7 Waves of SharePoint Governance' model is that 'Kaizen' (Continuous Improvement) exists both in isolation as a wave, but also as a fundamental part of all the other Governance elements. Continuous improvement is a key enabler, facilitating measurable, on-going organisational effectiveness improvements and enabling business led change through your SharePoint platform. As your vision evolves, as your business usage matures and as your organisation begins to innovate and expand its use of the platform, then your SharePoint implementation and Governance itself must also evolve.

...but don't take 3 months to react and deliver, in fact even 1 month may be too long!

The promise of Kaizen is in ensuring organisational capability to continually improve and of course IT's ability to deliver solutions aligned with business change delivered through 'small', agile projects, that produce measurable business outcomes and make a clear difference at an organisational level.

For me, one of the proven benefits from both an IT and business perspective of Governing and implementing in a Kaizen manner, is that it helps us to build an *'adaptive capacity'* into the organisation and instils the expectation of change and facilitates co-creation.

Wikipedia defines 'Adaptive Capacity' as:

"the capacity of a system [your organisation] to adapt
if the environment where the system exists is changing
[business landscape, economy, competitors, innovation
etc.]."

Some of the benefits of developing an 'Adaptive Capacity' in our organisations, that are relevant to our focus on SharePoint Governance, include:

- Organisational resilience
- Culture of co-creation
- Positive expectation of change
- Increased productivity.

These benefits and others derived from an organisation with an 'Adaptive Capacity' all help us to derive technology solutions that are fundamentally centred on the organisation and its stakeholders.

Textbooks on this subject talk extensively of culture, knowledge, transparency, systems thinking, complexity, emergent behaviour and self-organisation. All these are concepts that I have touched on previously in this Manifesto and none are directly to do with technology, although the value can certainly be amplified with platforms such as SharePoint.

Furthermore, I often talk, when appropriate, to organisations regarding a way of working which can foster Kaizen throughout the organisation, irrespective of technology and IT and that is the concept of the *'Learning Organisation'*.

First defined by Peter Senge (1994), Wikipedia defines the concept as follows:

"A learning organization is the term given to a company that facilitates the learning of its members and continuously transforms itself."

The concept was developed as a result of modern organisations being subjected to an ever increasing variety of pressures and should help facilitate them remaining competitive in their business environment.

A learning organisation has five main features:

- Systems thinking
- Personal mastery
- Mental models
- Shared vision
- Team learning.

Why is this relevant?

Well I hope it is fairly obvious, most of these features have already been mentioned throughout the Manifesto in various guises, so what the learning organisation teaches us from an organisational perspective, is fully in line with what we are trying to achieve from a technology governance perspective...

Phew!

Now I appreciate that this may feel like I'm just citing some big thinkers at you and to some extent that is exactly what I am doing!

But it's for a damn good reason...

I've experienced the power of these concepts, in facilitating 'change' in organisations and enabling IT departments to really add strategic value. But IT needs to be ready to bite the bullet and change the way that they work and deliver SharePoint projects.

The only way to save your SharePoint projects is to look outside of existing IT concepts...

What's wrong with delivering SharePoint projects using waterfall and governing in the old way, it has been working fine for us for years?

Seriously, has it been working, honestly?

Is the business happy?

Have you maximised the value out of your SharePoint platform?

Are the users happy?

Is your SharePoint team happy?

Do you have many outstanding requirements?

I expect that your answers aren't positive ones, there is a definite need for change, and I can sense it at the conferences, SharePoint user groups and the clients I engage with.

The challenges that Kaizen attempts to address are that for years, our users have felt ignored and insignificant. Their ways of working, structures and the business as a whole has changed, but their systems haven't changed, well at least not enough. Business users have gotten used to their old habits and have sadly become fond of their clunky, quirky systems. For us, this is a nightmare and equates to serious adoption and change challenges.

We don't want our business to have old, inefficient functionality and platforms, that have become stale and not seen as a strategic platform capable of supporting business change.

The business demands more than this, we are capable of delivering more than this, we need to work together and we need to adopt Kaizen to make it happen.

Adding some secret sauce

What's the secret to achieving an appropriate level of Governance for your SharePoint platform?

Hire **Soulsailor Consulting Ltd** to help you...

Only joking...

Actually I'm not joking, I've got to pay the mortgage, feed the family and buy shiny-geeky things!

In all seriousness, I think it makes sense to end this section of the Manifesto in the same way that the next section will start, by being **very practical**.

I briefly mentioned this earlier in the Manifesto, but I want to a little time to explain to you in more detail, the first steps I take with my clients, on the route to SharePoint Governance awesomeness.

I'm going to share with you my workshop approach, for clients starting out on disrupting their SharePoint Governance thinking and execution.

Don't tell anyone else about this OK?

Day 1

I run the first day of the engagement as a facilitative workshop using visual and 'collaborative play' techniques.

You should try to involve as many stakeholders from across IT and the business as you can get, ideally a minimum of 6 and a maximum of around 12, depending on how confident and experienced a facilitator you are. I certainly recommend being strong and delaying the workshop if you can't get engagement and commitment to the workshop from at least 6 people, of whom at least 2 are from the business.

Activity 1 - Education / buy them a copy of this book

As an optional kick-off activity, especially if this is a new project or the stakeholders don't know each other very well, I may use the Gamestorming technique *low-tech social network* to gain an understanding of roles, responsibilities, relationships and the organisational dynamics we have in the workshop. It's a great way to introduce people to working more interactively and usually results in some great insights.

The first thing I always do, is go through some overview of slides about why SharePoint Governance is so complex and needs to move away from its focus on IT, what Governance really is and an overview of the 7 waves. I have lots of examples of similar slides on my Slideshare channel (http://www.slideshare.net/soulsailor).

Depending on the engagement or the level of relationship with the client etc. I will often then spend some time exploring and documenting the current landscape in the context of the project or platform we are interested in. Typically I use a visual technique such as Innovation Games, *Spider Web*, *Sailboat* or perhaps visual facilitation of some kind. Alternatively, mind-mapping or dialogue mapping are other effective techniques to use at this stage.

Activity 2 - Vision

As you may expect, whatever I'm told, I will pretty much always spend some time running a group activity using the Gamestorming technique *Cover Story*. This technique, as described earlier in the Manifesto, helps get a shared understanding and commitment around the vision that our SharePoint Governance is steering us towards.

Those activities and all the ensuing conversations will normally take us to lunch time.

Activity 3 - Governance Audit

The afternoon is focussed on getting into the detail of the Governance needed by the client to achieve their goals. My most common approach to this is to create a visual canvas representing each of the 7 waves, up on a large wall. I then take a two-pass facilitation approach, using 2 different coloured post-it notes to identify what Governance is currently in place and then, based on what we know so far, what Governance is required or recommended. In both these cases we are looking for input in the form of:

- People, teams, groups, roles
- Processes
- Culture
- Legislation, compliance, law
- Technology, tools, platforms.

As this exercise is both active i.e. the participants have to identify something, write it down and place it on the visual canvas and facilitated i.e. I am prompting, probing and exploring everything that is discussed, the session is very hard work, and is usually very illuminating for all concerned. As the session evolves, there very quickly emerges a clear view of the current state of their Governance and the high-level view of what needs to be done in each area.

Depending on time and the clarity of the next steps identified in the previous exercise, I may optionally finish the workshop with a planning exercise, to work with the attendees to identify the initial next steps, order, priorities etc. There's a number of techniques that can be used here, I favour using Innovation Games *Remember the Future*, but other techniques work just as well.

Day 2

Activity 4 - Identify Governance Actions and Recommendations

The second day of the engagement is spent pulling together the workshop activities, outputs, recommendations and next steps etc. into a written report. I try to incorporate as many of the visuals from the workshop as possible and minimise the written word as much as is appropriate. The purpose of the output is to document the key aspects:

- Organisational position
- Vision
- Current state of Governance
- Next steps and recommendations.

The report does not need to be huge and does not need to be full of consultancy speak. The contents of the document should be in a format that ensures that everyone involved in the project is on the same page and that the path that the project team needs to steer towards its vision is clearly stated and broken down in sufficient detail to be of value.

Day 3 onwards

Activity 5 - Get delivering

Finally, although for most this is the start of a long journey, we can either let the client get on with it themselves or support and actively participate in the creation, implementation and on-going delivery of the SharePoint Governance.

Typically, from a consultant perspective, this part of the engagement can last anything from 5 days to 20 days, obviously for the client it's an infinite process of continuous improvement!

That's my broad approach to kick-starting the Governance disruption process with my clients; I hope you find it useful. As with all things in Governance, my approach and the techniques I use are evolving, it would be wrong if I wasn't in a constant cycle of Kaizen wouldn't it?

Governance Duct Tape

Will you take the Red or Blue Pill?

"This is your last chance.

After this point, there is no turning back.

*You take the **blue pill - this story ends**, you wake up in your office and believe whatever you want to believe.*

*You take the **red pill - you stay here in Governance Wonderland**, and I show you how deep the rabbit hole goes..."*

That quote is based on one from the film The Matrix as Morpheus explains the only choices left for Neo.

So, before we move on, it's time for **you** to make a choice.

Don't screw it up.

Think hard about the reality you want to live in, the reality that you want your SharePoint projects to prosper within and the reality of your business or organisation.

We've talked at length through this manifesto, about the origins, challenges, theory and some of the practical aspects of SharePoint Governance in this new world that I hope we can envisage together... I'm really glad and humbled that you've stuck with me for this long.

Let's be clear.

There's really no bloody point in me wasting your or my time, explaining on these final pages, how to apply SharePoint Governance effectively in your organisation, if all you're going to do is put this book back on the shelf (virtual or physical) and maintain the status quo.

You have to commit, here and now.

Ask yourself, is this your dogma? (http://en.wikipedia.org/wiki/Dogma)

Do you feel the SharePoint Governance fire in your belly?

Do you have the energy to change your part of your SharePoint world?

Can you feel yourself being engulfed and swept along towards your vision by the seven waves of SharePoint Governance?

Is this the path you really want to take?

Will you take the Red or the Blue Pill?

Decide now.

Make a Choice

OK it's **"choose your own adventure"** time.

Option 1

If you just swallowed the Blue pill then go back to **page 1**.

Either I didn't explain it well or you didn't get it or this book really isn't for you, sorry. Try reading it again, just like some movies, it can take a few viewings before you really get the plot.

Option 2

If you didn't swallow any pill then get in touch with me now. (http://bit.ly/TalkToSoulsailor)

Let's meet up or have a call and let me help you choose the right path.

Option 3

If you just swallowed the Red pill then welcome to my fantastic world!

Please read on and change your SharePoint Governance world.

Applying Governance

Phew...

That was close...

Good call my friend.

> *"Be the change you want to see in the world"* - Mahatma
> Gandhi

I think Gandhi was a pretty clever bloke; the title of the chapter reflects a famous quote he may have once uttered when he was looking at all the failed technology projects in the world...

Well maybe that wasn't what inspired that quote, but it's pertinent to the points I want to get across in my final words of this Manifesto.

Actually, being honest it seems that Ghandi probably didn't even say that quote, which is a real shame.

The New York Times:

http://www.nytimes.com/2011/08/30/opinion/falser-words-were-never-spoken.html?_r=0)

states that the closest verifiable remark we have from Gandhi that is related to these over used words is this:

> *"If we could change ourselves, the tendencies in the world would also change. As a man changes his own nature, so does the attitude of the world change towards him.*
>
> *...We need not wait to see what others do."*

Which isn't quite so succinct, but it is still pretty cool.

So how do we change our SharePoint world? How do you actually implement this stuff, maintain control and value and still have time to relax and enjoy life?

This is where **you** are really going to have to start putting in the effort, doing the work, blood, sweat, tears, frustration, pain and continual challenges...

This is where the disruption starts for real!

I hope that this is where the real fun, enjoyment and satisfaction can be experienced.

If we take the previous 140 or so pages as being the preparation and the ammunition for this Governance fight, then the next set of pages amounts to the strategy and weapons that you can use to take this battle into your business... and win!

Our Governance strategy, unsurprisingly based upon the 7 waves, is going to cover three key areas of attack:

- **Governance Content** (Documents)
- **Governance Decision Making** (Boards)
- **In-line Governance** (sign-posting and steering).

All this should be facilitated and amplified by a concept called *'Work Out Loud'* or *Observable Work.*

This term was coined by a guy named Bryce Williams and you can read more about it in his blog post: **"When will we Work Out Loud? Soon!"** (Williams, B., 2010, http://bit.ly/WorkOutLoud)and other writings across the web that he references.

For now, all I think you need to know is the fundamentals, which Bryce articulates as:

Working Out Loud = Observable Work + Narrating Your Work

Fundamentally this means that we should visualise our work so people can *observe* and *narrate our work*, so that it can tell its story and articulate its context and impact.

In the context of on-going Governance, it means that we should get it [our Governance] out there amongst the stakeholders, business users, SharePoint techies and management.

But in my mind that's only half the story.

It's great that more people have access to Governance content and can see what we are trying to achieve. That's great, but to be truly awesome it's not just visualising and 'working out loud' that we need to do, for me that facilitates an opportunity for value, but does not necessarily help us drive action and engagement.

I would take Bryce's work one step further and state that we need to **socialise** our work to really makes a difference.

My interpretation of Bryce's 'Work out loud' formula is therefore:

Working Out Loud = Observable Work + Narrating Your Work x Socialise the work

When we socialise our Governance we are being transparent, letting people into our world (which let's face it, shouldn't be our [IT] world anyway) and inviting them to participate, engage and join in.

This is the key, this is what I think makes a huge difference and is directly linked to effective change management and positive user adoption. If we have an organisation where we are implementing SharePoint, which as we discussed earlier is going to change the way they all work, then engaging them, on an on-going basis is going to foster a culture of *co-creation* and *adaptive capacity*.

The following sections of this Manifesto will, I hope, arm you with sufficient guidance and steer (no apologise for the pun) to go ahead and disrupt the SharePoint Governance thinking and practice within your organisation.

Remember this is all based on what I have heard, thought, discussed and experienced over many years. Even now as I am writing this Manifesto and working with new clients consulting and implementing Governance, new things, ideas, thinking and practices are emerging.

Take what we have discussed, learnt and explored so far and use it as **you** want to, as a starting point for your Governance adventure.

It looks like you already have the passion and I am proud and honoured to be amongst you...

Governance Content

Look around your office, look around your team's SharePoint site, where is 'the Governance' stored?

I'd anticipate a significant proportion of you will be reaching for search or the dusty bookshelf or filling cabinet looking for the 'Governance document'.

For a lot of people, Governance is represented by a large document stored somewhere and watched night and day by the IT guardians of your organisation.

The audit trail of when it was last updated signified by:

- The depth of dust on the cover
- Tracing the fingerprints clearly visible in said dust, from the employee who retired two years ago
- 'Search' can't find it or finds lots of different documents called 'Governance'
- The last modified property is before you joined the organisation!

If you asked a random business user or your executive board where the SharePoint Governance was kept, or whether it even existed, they would likely shrug their shoulders and have no idea.

Things *may be better* than this in your organisation, you may direct me to a document library or file server or even suggest a quick search would be an effective approach.

But what would I find?

- **Nothing...**
- **Multiple versions?** I assume the latest updated one is the right one to look at, right?

- **Locked down security**, hell can I even see the document if I search?
- **No audit trail**
- **Only IT content?** You're going to change this though aren't you?
- **Some Information Governance content perhaps?** Excellent, you're starting to go in the right direction!

The results of what you as an organisation have, in terms of Governance documentation, are likely to be as varied and diverse as the snowflakes falling outside my window as I write this section!

> **Listen folks, you don't need a Governance document anymore...**
>
> **Delete it, rip it up, burn it, sacrifice it to your gods...**

Sigh.

I would **love** to be as bold and confident in our collective future to be able to state that. The reality is that for at least the foreseeable future, Governance documents aren't going away. They simply can't just disappear, as our maturity, culture and ways of working just don't support what would be a rapid and beautiful demise of the Governance document. It is also the only auditable hard proof of Governance evidence we have, if we were to be challenged.

But we can start to challenge our approach to Governance documentation.

Consider the following top 10 steps for moving towards the new order of Governance content:

1. Think content not document

2. Become more visual, lots more visual, in fact you just **can't** be too visual, think about the impact and power of things like Commonn Craft's 'explainer videos' (http://www.commoncraft.com) or the RSA Animate series (http://www.thersa.org/events/rsaanimate)

3. Think of your audiences, you have more than one, it's not just about the IT team and impressing your boss that you're doing something

4. Break it down and use the 7 waves as an initial structure

5. Align it to the vision and if you don't have a vision then make that your next priority!

6. In all but 'IT Assurance' avoid using technical terms, think about your audience, for the most part you shouldn't be talking about technology features so this will be easuier than you think

7. Use a wiki

8. Be open by default

9. Tell everyone, share with everyone, ask for input and feedback from everyone

10. Think about 'Lean principles' and focus on quality, clarity and brevity not showboating your technical knowledge

11. *My book, my rules.* Evolve, don't worry about mistakes, don't stress about the gaps, once you start to 'work out loud' your Governance will evolve and become as complete as it needs to be.

So what do we write and sketch in order to create our new and shiny 'Governance Document', taking into account what we have discussed over the preceding pages?

Before we go into capturing the details, think outside your technology platform.

Ant's Tip:
Start by facilitating and capturing the Vision

If you think about it everything we do from a Governance perspective should *flow from the vision*, so it makes sense to start here and then the reality is that I don't (and neither should you) care about what comes next.

This is **your organisations Governance** content, what makes sense to you is cool by me, just get on and do it.

What I will say though is that however you structure your content, you need to think carefully about the flow of information and how that differs between your different audiences.

Some of the most common Governance audiences types I have found and utilise include:

- Senior Management
- End User
- Power User
- Tummeler
- IT Platform
- IT Development
- SharePoint C o E.

Ant's Tip:

Use 'Empathy Maps' to target content accurately for your Governance audiences.

If you want to do this properly in your organisation, consider a spot of 'empathy mapping' for the key Governance audiences to really identify the content, interactions and behaviours they need from you. Ask your friendly UX expert (or me) for help in running an Empathy Map session and really getting to grips with how to effectively create, target and socialise your Governance content.

What else do we need to consider?

We have a vision, we understand our Governance audiences that we want to target...

I guess now all we need is create the content.

This may be the easy bit, but it is certainly the area where most controversy lies.

Why?

Because there is no one format or template for creating your Governance content.

To some extent you are on your own... Sorry, but every organisation is different.

The knowledge and guidance you want to impart may be structured the same, may at the core be pretty similar, but different organisations and different audiences can consume information in very different ways. This could include a plethora of combinations of the following:

- Lists
- Sketches
- Diagrams
- Prose
- Processes
- Tables.

It's up to you how you present this stuff depending on your organisational preferences and culture. I won't leave you completely in the dark though, here's a candle to shed a little light on what the possibilities are and what I have had most success using so far...

The intention of your Governance content is to steer the use of your technology platform, SharePoint in this case, towards a vision. For this reason I recommend embedding the SharePoint Governance content within all your other SharePoint content, wherever that is -

help pages, tutorials, support contacts etc. That way the Governance content contributes to the overall SharePoint body of knowledge within your organisation.

However, there is a note of caution, it would be good practice to **not** store your Governance material relating to disaster recovery and other technically sensitive material on the platform they are designed to govern.

Typically when I work with clients we implement a wiki structure with the Vision at the 'top' and then the seven waves as the main levels of the overall 'Governance wiki' structure.

Underneath these main wiki pages, the rest of the content can naturally be presented and structured in whatever way makes sense.

Just to clarify the type of content you may want to be thinking about in the 7 waves structure:

- **Business Alignment** - This area is especially for focussing on the business aspects, Vision, definitions, measurable business outcomes, business alignment and where the platform fits in the overall business architecture
- **IT Assurance** - This is all of your infrastructure and SharePoint platform related content, you won't find business users looking at this stuff, knock yourself out and go appropriately geeky! Obviously if your using SharePoint Online this section will be very very light!
- **Project Governance** - This should contain content around how you will manage the implementation, stakeholders, managing changes and anything else related to the delivery of the platform
- **Information Governance** - This area is going to cover everything from information security, content types, metadata, user experience, retention periods etc. so there will definitely be a mixed audience; you won't be able to avoid talking

features and a level of geek-speak, but keep to a minimum and talk in more business parlance

- **Change Management and Adoption** - Here's where all the content around embedding the solution into the business will go; including help, list of change champions, cultural aspects, business initiatives the platform is aligned to and anything else that will help support the business in adopting this change. In some cases this may even be guidance around moving from one platform to another in the form of very targetted user guides and help
- **Social Business** - Look at including content that includes guidance on using social features, social business strategy, cultural aspects and ways of working. You may find that you need to raise these new ideals to the executive or reviewing and amending existing policies
- **Kaizen** - Include the processes and procedures for requesting changes and enhancements, how to engage with the SharePoint Centre of Excellence, where and how work on the platform is visualised and socialised, how the business can become involved in the evolution of the platform.

On the whole, as you can see above, most content in your Governance should be written in a way that it can be consumed by the business.

So now you should have in mind a simple, logical and hierarchical structure that supports the flow of knowledge required by our Governance audiences. How do we represent our Governance thoughts, processes and policies within this?

- KISS (Keep It Simple Silly) - Simplicity, brevity and focus, don't ramble
- Use explanatory text and bullets where it makes sense and adds value

- I try to use lots of diagrams, typically using sketches 'drawn' in Autodesk Sketchbook Pro, but Visio or Balsamiq are great alternatives. You should also consider the 'Common Craft' and RSA Animate styles of explaining ideas and thoughts
- Tables
- RACI (Responsible, Accountable, Consulted, Informed), discussed later

Ant's Tip:

My diagram creation process usually consists of a brainwave (train, plane, shower, walking the dog), very rough sketches in an actual physical paper-based sketchbook and then clarification and tidying-up (but it still looks like a sketch) in Autodesk Sketchbook Pro.

Yes, but **what** actually goes in the document, what words and diagrams do I normally use, what's the best practice...

STOP!

I am not, I repeat not, going to write your Governance content for you, and here are three reasons out of many as to why:

- It will wildly differ depending on what type of solutions you are doing (Intranet, Extranet, Social, Collaboration, Knowledge Management, Business App Etc.)
- I need some Consulting revenue of my own!
- Governance content is emergent, if I told you what to write here on these pages, by next week things will have moved on.

How else can I help you on this journey towards your Governance vision?

I'll talk about RACI charts in a later section, they're pretty cool for documenting Governance ownership and responsibility.

I probably over emphasise making sure the business users and all consumers of my Governance content are damn clear about the *definitions*, but this is one area that is easily resolved and prevents a hell of a lot of hassle further down the line.

If you don't believe me then let's take the classic reason for implementing SharePoint... We want to '**collaborate**'.

Now, do you, your stakeholders, the business users and the executive board **all** have the same perspective as to what *collaborate* means?

- IT think it means **SharePoint Team Sites**
- The business user thinks it is a **File sharing software like Dropbox**
- The executive board thought you were implementing **a room with lots of whiteboards and free coffee, tea and fizzy drinks**.

So you see, we really do need to get nailed down and 'work out loud' the core definitions of key 'words' in our SharePoint platform. This is content that, along with the Vision, should be flowing through everyone's 'grey matter'.

Another area that I think is highly valuable and infinitely adaptable is to document visually or in a table, your **Governance Principles**.

I tend to use three elements to this and make extra effort to make this content and engaging as I can:

1. Governance Principle
2. Implication
3. Guidance.

An Example could be:

Governance Principle This is the behaviour that we are trying to encourage or discourage. Be succinct and frankly, pretty blunt!

Content, sites and all information on the SharePoint platform will be created 'Public', 'Open' and searchable by default.

Implication Explain to the reader what we are trying to achieve through this principle or what we are trying to avoid.

Consider the security, access and findability requirements of any sites, content or social interactions you make on content within the SharePoint platform.

Guidance Where I can, I usually try to keep this light-hearted and easy to understand. This is your opportunity to steer behaviour.

Think first! Create second...

From this point onwards, just write, sketch, record whatever you feel you need to. The acid test is always whether you have *just enough* content to:

- Articulate why the hell the platform is here in the first place
- Keep your business users and IT team out of trouble
- Comply with organisational and legal Governance, compliance and legislation
- Facilitate the business in maximising business value from the platform
- Supporting your people.

Relatively speaking its simple, yeh?

Governance Decision Making

Just like I'd like to burn all the Governance documentation, I'd also love to nuke Governance boards, but the business world has not evolved enough to let that be a reality.

Instead let's reimagine the role of Governance boards, make them appropriate and get them actually doing some freakin' work!

My perspective is that whether you are small organisation or a huge multi-national, it makes sense to establish Governance boards of some kind.

These Governance Boards should all have a clear level of responsibility, undertake scheduled and proactive activities and have the authority (and passion) to make decisions.

My current thinking and recommendation is for most organisations to formally have 3 levels, notice I said levels not hierarchy or specific boards.

These 3 levels are tasked with covering the following:

- **Strategic Governance** - Responsible for the big scary organisation-level impact decisions, such as let's use SharePoint for Knowledge Management or other decisions that have organisational impact
- **Functional Governance** - Responsible for the on-going business alignment and maximising the value of the platform. This level makes the less strategic decisions such as changes in Information Governance, new business projects etc.
- **Day-2-day Governance** - This is an interesting layer which we will discuss further when we talk about In-Line Governance. Suffice to say this level deals with the everyday Governance challenges, issues and changes such as proactive maintenance of the term store (metadata), maintaining search configuration or supporting users in business alignment.

For some larger organisations, such as those with country specific IT capability or very specific geographically based business units, there may even be requirement for 'local' country level governance. In my experience, this is relevant at both the Functional and the Day-2-day Governance Board levels, however I recommend that there is only one Strategic level Board.

The following images articulate a small sample of some of the ideal elements for each of the Governance levels. The roles you see here may be delivered by multiple people, such as the Senior Business Owners and an individual may serve on several roles:

STRATEGIC GOVERNANCE TEAM ROLES

Role	Responsibilities and Tasks	Required Skills
Executive Sponsor	Responsible for ownership and communication of SharePoint vision and strategy	• Strategic planning • Leadership • Visioning • Innovation
Senior Business Owner(s)	Responsible for owning and directing a specific piece of the portal, relevant to their business unit, department, or team.	• Strategic planning • Visioning • Leadership • Innovation
Etc.	Etc.	
Etc.	Etc.	

Example Strategic Governance Team Roles

FUNCTIONAL GOVERNANCE TEAM ROLES

Role	Responsibilities and Tasks	Required Skills
Business Owner(s)	Responsible for owning and directing a specific piece of the portal, relevant to their business unit, department, or team.	• Strategic planning • Visioning • Innovation
SharePoint Architect	Responsible for translating business needs addressed by the Strategy Team into initiatives for the portal and coordinating SharePoint Administrator efforts. • Review business requirements • Design the initial architecture for successful development • Provide architectural guidance to development • Lead consulting team for initial release • Work with the Infrastructure Team to develop infrastructure and operation best practices • Work with System Administrators to develop best practices	• SharePoint Architecture • Business Analysis • Systems analysis • Networking • IT research • Strategic planning • Resource planning
SharePoint Programme Manager	Responsible for delivering SharePoint infrastructure and functional projects and ensuring the Governance Plan is followed as part of the delivery process • Manage tactical teams and project risks, and escalate incidents to the business as necessary • Ensure all project deliverables deliver the intended business value • Ensure all project deliverables are completed and report progress to the strategy Board. • Ensure the strategy Board propose realistic goals and plan accordingly.	• Programme / portfolio management • Project management • Strategic planning • Group leadership • Resource planning
Business Analyst	Responsible for communicating with the business to gather requirements and translating them into business solutions.	• Financial analysis • Technical understanding • Facilitation Skills
Change Manager	Business focussed people with a broad range of business skills and high-level SharePoint capability, able to engage end-users, business stakeholders and executive teams to help facilitate business change through the SharePoint platform	• Broad SharePoint Knowledge • Strategic planning • Change Management • Leadership • Visioning • Innovation

Example Functional Governance Team Roles

DAY-2-DAY GOVERNANCE TEAM ROLES

Role	Responsibilities and Tasks	Required Skills
Technical Authority	The key people in the group who have a deep technical and architectural skills in addition to being able to have grown up sensible business conversations	• SharePoint Architecture • Systems analysis • IT research • Strategic planning
SharePoint Architect	Responsible for translating business needs addressed by the Strategy Team into initiatives for the portal and coordinating SharePoint Administrator efforts. • Gather initial business requirements • Design the initial architecture for successful development • Provide architectural guidance to development • Lead consulting team for initial release • Work with the Infrastructure Team to develop infrastructure and operation best practices • Work with System Administrators to develop best practices	• Systems analysis • Networking • IT research • Strategic planning • Resource planning
Subject Matter Experts	A range of people with deep skills in specific areas of the technology platforms. Examples being, Search, Collaboration, Forms, Records Management etc. Again these roles should be able to have grown up sensible business conversations	• Deep SharePoint knowledge in a specific area
Business Analyst	Responsible for communicating with the business to gather requirements and translating them into business solutions. They should utilise more collaborative, emergent and facilitative techniques to engage the business and articulate measurable business outcomes	• Financial analysis • Technical understanding of SharePoint • Business Analysis • Facilitation
End-User Training	A role capable of training end-users both on core SharePoint functionality and customised business solutions as well as playing a fundamental part in change management activities.	• Training • Facilitation • Broad SharePoint Knowledge
Change Agents	Business focussed people with a broad range of business skills and high-level SharePoint capability, able to engage end-users, business stakeholders and executive teams to help facilitate business change through the SharePoint platform	• Broad SharePoint Knowledge • Strategic planning • Change Management • Leadership • Visioning • Innovation

Example Day 2 Day Governance Team Roles

Articulating the structure and responsibilities of your Governance Boards also works well really represented as a RACI table.

I have now started to add an extra element, the letter 'P' for 'Proactive' to the method, in order to align closer with my expectations:

- R - Responsible [the doer]
- A - Accountable [the arse kicker]
- C - Consulted [the adviser]
- I - Informed [the impacted]
- *P - Proactive [the good stuff].*

Thinking about who should be proactively working on your SharePoint business platform adds a unique and extremely valuable perspective to on-going Governance.

In-line Governance

Point #1 is that this has nothing to do with in-line roller-skates!

In-line Governance in the context of this Manifesto is **anything** that helps the business users (and yourselves) stay in sync with your Governance aspirations.

If we go back to the start of the Manifesto, you'll remember that we talked about taking Governance back to its first principle:

To Steer...

If we are going to be steering towards our organisations Vision, sometimes that's a long, long way away and we need some help along the way to keep you on the right tack (not a typo as many reviewers though! I meant 'tack' in a nautical sense) and pointing the platform in the right direction. That is what 'In-line Governance' is all about. It is the light-hand on the tiller that helps correct us when we go off-course and makes life just a little bit easier for us all.

So how do we deliver in-line Governance? In order to be effective I think that this element needs approaching in two primary ways:

- Technology - Yes we do need help from the robots
- People - Don't rely on just robots!

In the next two sections, I will articulate some of the key approaches to in-line Governance that I have implemented or seen in action and believe are effective.

The sections are, shall we say a little biased i.e. there are only a couple of approaches in the 'technology' section, although they can be very powerful and within the 'people' section there are a shed-load of approaches and ideas and that is only the tip of the iceberg.

I don't apologise for this bias!

Technology

So far I have only really come across three effective ways to embed SharePoint Governance in your organisation:

1. **Technology** - Governance Tools
2. **Content** - Sign-posting within SharePoint
3. **Motivation** - Gamification.

I'm seeing a real surge in the quality and effectiveness of Governance tools across SharePoint management, reporting, analysis etc. These have a tendency to be focussed more towards IT Assurance and Information Governance aspects of the 7 Wave model, but they are, as part of a wider approach, very useful. In fact there are a couple of vendors that are probably leaps apart from the rest of the bunch, with some pretty sophisticated offerings. I've mentioned some of the key vendors elsewhere in this Manifesto, you won't go far wrong with them.

Using these tools, we can very quickly gain insights into usage, security and start to gain some control over our content and solution usage, but for the most part they are retrospective tools, so on their own they aren't all that beneficial long-term.

That said, please don't dismiss these. Find what works from the handful of awesome players in this areaand if this isn't enough then get in touch with me and I'll point you in the right direction.

So now you've installed some technology, you have, I hope, got a much clearer picture of where things are with your platform?

What next?

Well I'm going to recommend you now go and have a real good, detailed look at your content.

No, not the businesses content, but the stuff that you can...

shhhhh! *[Stealthily insert "...to help 'steer' your users towards the vision.."].*

I see this 'content' falling in to two very overlapping, but I think useful to discriminate, focus areas:

1. Sign-posts within SharePoint to specific Governance Content ('Work out loud' as we discussed earlier)
2. Sign-posts within SharePoint that give Context (Why? Vision etc.)

The first method is pretty easy to implement, it's kind of like Help content for Governance. In my head, these signposts, maybe even use a sign-post icon, should be on every 'page' or 'app'. Their purpose is to direct the user to any relevant Governance content. Why would we do this? Well here's my list of reasons:

- Help explain in business terms, why the metadata exists
- Articulate in business terms, why the security is as it is
- Explain in business terms the reason for the workflow.

The second method is more difficult to execute well, but is equally valid and important and is focussed around articulating how business functionality within your technical solution aligns to the Vision i.e. you are proactively informing the user 'Why'.

This can be achieved through a number of routes, including, but not limited to:

- Visible metadata about the reason for the page, site, library or app
- Hover text explaining 'Why'
- Content (News, articles, text, documents etc.) articulating context or 'Why'

- Seeding 'content' i.e. including content in some way that 'behaves' and has the same attributes as you wish the users to create.

Although this is one of my favourite techniques, it is also something that can get really overused, remember:

Ant's Tip:

In-line Governance content should inform and steer, it shouldn't be overbearing or distracting. Think '...light hand on the tiller...'

Lastly in the more technology-based aspects of In-line Governance we have the misused, misinterpreted and often misrepresented *Miss Whatever-her-name-is...* (Sorry that last bit was from a line from a Hothouse Flowers track called 'I'm Sorry' that I love). As I was saying, the last area that is much more complex and challenging to implement and get right, is the area called **Gamification**.

Gamification **isn't** [just] about playing and having fun.

If you think Gamification is about giving people badges, points and having a shiny leaderboard, then you are misinformed.

The true definition of Gamification is something like game thinking, game mechanics and gaming techniques used in non-game contexts in order to engage users and solve problems.

For me an important addition to that typical definition is '**to motivate and reward**', basically in the context of SharePoint Governance, Gamification's role is solely in change management and user adoption in order to steer people and encourage them to use the platform to achieve the business goals.

My simple test for whether you have implemented Gamification for the right reasons is as follows:

Can you really answer any of these questions?

- What [business] behaviours are you trying to change?
- What [business] behaviours are you trying to reward?
- What [business] behaviours are you trying to sustain?
- What difference are you trying to make to the business?
- How does the Gamification 'thing' you are implementing align to your Vision?

Basically, if you are not trying to change behaviours, sustain positive behaviours and/or reward then you are probably looking at Gamification for the wrong reasons.

If you can't answer yes to at least one of the above questions then you are, I suspect, using Gamification more as a buzz word and to get on the gamification gravy train, than for the good of your organisation and the SharePoint platform.

Hmmm. Notice that all words that begin with 'G' need to be done for the right reasons? Think about it!

Assuming that you are going to use game thinking, game mechanics and gaming techniques within your SharePoint platform for the right reasons, then how does this work for our on-going Governance quest? (See what I did there?!)

There are unsurprisingly two main options:

1. Buy some Gamification software
2. Craft your own gamified functionality.

At this point in time, I really don't know or care which you pick.

The very few vendors that are out there with SharePoint Gamification solutions are all pretty good. I would look more closely at those that have already released this stuff for consumers and doing well before coming to our SharePoint world. And please don't forget to make sure that the functionality they offer and even more importantly the customisations available will accurately meet your business goals. You mustn't take shortcuts here, otherwise you are just delivering a fancy bit of technology with no real value and I hope that by now you'll know that that isn't a good thing? Remember what that's called? **SharePoint Celery**.

So to finish off this short section on Gamification, why are we using these techniques?

It's because we want to:

- Encourage good Governance
- Reward those that are following our Governance steer
- Sustain all the behaviours and cultural changes that support our Vision.

The only way to really change behaviours, supported by Gamification is:

- Make sure that people understand why we need to change i.e. the difference it will make
- It should be achievable and follow i.e. small incremental changes are easier to swallow than large scale big, bad, scary change
- Ensure that your users, the organisations employees, see and can quantify both personal and organisational value from doing so.

This is an area that can and really should be discussed at much more length and in much more detail than this brief overview. I hope that this is enough for you to see the value in 'doing' gamification, for the right reasons. To be honest I'm just skimming the surface with my own learning, I've read some content and I did an on-line course at Coursera about the topic which was pretty awesome.

But remember, with any new concept there are dangers:

- Are you encouraging the right behaviours for the long-term?
- What are the risks if it doesn't work?
- What if it works too well? *People focussing on the gamified elements or just can you scale up the platform and your team to meet the demands of much more content, social interactions and innovative feature requests?*
- Are the techniques you are using sustainable?

Good luck, I'm betting on Gamification **and** you guys to be the next SharePoint revolution!

People

People, people, people...

You may remember I mentioned earlier in the Manifesto that:

SharePoint Projects are People Projects

I've also mentioned that we need 'people' to amplify our Governance messages, thinking and ways of working.

So how do we get 'people', some of whom will never have heard of SharePoint, most won't give a damn about it and let's face it I don't blame them and then there's the minority, you guys who have an interest in SharePoint, Governance and what I'm writing about here?

To me this is the most important, disruptive and powerful aspect of embedding Governance within your organisation. Without this 'element' it isn't going to happen, or rather you may seem some progress, but this will ultimately be unsustainable.

I think organisation and employee culture, behaviour and mechanics etc. are grossly underestimated in our SharePoint world. Combined with the Gamification elelemts that I mentioned previously, this is in my opinion the **next big thing** in SharePoint, assuming the last big thing was 'social'.

This is a difficult section to write and an even more difficult section to write well, as this whole genre of thinking is **HUGE!** So I'll give it a go and try to at least give you some insights into areas you need to explore and research and practical ideas that I think are effective in at least starting to turn our SharePoint and technology projects into business and change projects.

In my eyes there are three major initiatives that I want you to put on the kanban board to address... soon!

- Centre of Excellence
- Tummelers
- Power Users.

Together, these three approaches will really help you to positively disrupt the way your organisation engages with the SharePoint platform.

But before we go into these properly, have you ever thought about your organisation? You know the people that touch your solution in some way, have you ever thought about them as people rather than users or employees?

No?

Neither had I until recently, take a minute now, put the Manifesto down, don't lose your page, and try this:

- Shut your eyes
- Visualise a person in your organisation from a different [business] department
- Classify that person in terms of using your SharePoint solution
- Now think about that person's actual job role
- Now think about that person's motivation for doing that job role well
- Now think about that person's motivation to be at work
- What pressures are they under? Promotion, performance reviews, long hours, staff, disciplinary, take-overs, the boss etc.
- Now think about their home life... Mortgage, health, family, divorce, party-time, holidays, retirement etc.
- Now open your eyes and pick up the Manifesto.

Does it concern you that this may well have been the first time you actually thought about your users as *real people* in the context of your SharePoint Governance?

Time to panic?

Yes I think so...

But you're not alone, don't worry yourself too much, but please do something about it now!

The users of your SharePoint platform, those people being steered by your Governance, are real flesh and bones with their own motivations, skills, drivers, influences etc.

To really dive deep into this area then I recommend you read Daniel Pink's seminal book 'Drive' (Pink, D., 2011, http://bit.ly/PinkBookDrive).

Daniel Pink describes people's 'drive' and motivation arising from:

- Autonomy
- Mastery
- Purpose

So it is these attributes that we should seek to support through cultural and organisational changes as well as via technology and the support and governance we implement.

There are all manner of ideas, concepts and approaches to people in organisations and how they should or shouldn't be structured, how to facilitate culture and foster innovation and all the awesomeness.

I do think as SharePoint people this is an area of knowledge we could all drastically improve on.

Concepts like:

- Working out loud
- You weren't meant to have a boss
- Honeycomb organisational structure
- Rightshifting
- Complexity theory
- Organisational theory based on the behaviour of ants (not me)
- The Fifth discipline
- Chaordic organisations
- Open innovation
- Tribal leadership.

Wow, even in the few seconds it took for me to write out only a handful of organisational and behavioural 'ideas' my head has nearly exploded and I've read or am currently reading books and whitepapers on some of those topics!

I don't want your heads to explode, that really wouldn't make for a good book review...

But I do want you to open your eyes to a world, maybe even a galaxy, of thinking that has **absolutely nothing to do with SharePoint [technology] but absolutely everything to do with SharePoint [in your organisation]**.

SharePoint Centre of Excellence

Let's start this section with some thoughts on techniques or concept naming... To my mind 'names of things' are pretty much irrelevant, not that they don't have meaning, more that I really don't give a crap what you call things as long as in your organisational context, everyone has a shared understanding.

So with that let's launch into an awesome concept that is commonly called the **SharePoint Centre of Excellence**.

Although I use this term a lot, it does have an air of elitism which I don't like, so here are some other ideas of what you can call this 'thing':

- SharePoint Family
- SharePoint Guild
- SharePoint Tribe
- SharePoint Centre for Excellence
- SharePoint Clan.

Let's face it even 'SharePoint Team' will probably suffice, what is important is the vision, role, culture and behaviours of this 'group'.

So this group, the SharePoint Centre of Excellence, is a key supporting and facilitating structure for the individuals, teams and departments within your organisation.

I usually define it as an 'extended team' that will enable your organisation to focus on ensuring that the SharePoint platform is fully aligned to their business vision.

The SharePoint Centre of Excellence will enable the creation of solutions that make best used of the technologies available, within the context of the SharePoint platform. It will facilitate business users to build knowledge, experience, maturity and capability with the confidence and support of the SharePoint Centre of Excellence.

Why an 'extended team'? Well the main reason is that I see this 'body' as being made up of, at least the following groups:

- The SharePoint Centre of Excellence
- Development and technology partners (internal and external)
- Governance boards
- Tummelers
- Power Users.

As you can see this is very clearly **not just** a well-defined team within an organisational hierarchy, it is significantly more.

Responsibilities and Activities

The responsibilities of the SharePoint Centre of Excellence can be broken down into three primary categories of activities and responsibilities, which I will expand upon in a moment:

- **Proactive** – Should be done continually by the Centre of Excellence
- **Business** – Either driven by or required by the business
- **Platform** – For the benefit of the SharePoint Centre of Excellence or to drive further value from the platform.

To help you craft your own version of this powerful group, here are some ideas of what these areas may get up to.

It's very important that the SharePoint Centre of Excellence is proactive and these activities should include a mix of technology and softer skills:

- Promote Success through workshops, case studies and evangelism
- Monitor and audit site collection creating and usage

- Monitor and tune Search
- Monitor and tune Enterprise Keywords
- Engage with the business
- Look for opportunities for both business innovation and business process reengineering
- Build a business community around the platform and solutions.

The business activities should include at least:

- Acting as a single point of contact for everything related to SharePoint
- Undertaking requirements facilitation
- Managing the Change Process
- User Training
- Measuring value and Return On Investment (ROI)
- Help teams and individuals discover opportunities for business value from the implemented solutions and the platform
- Facilitate teams developing a shared understanding and shared commitment on their use of the SharePoint Platform.

From a platform perspective, activities are more targeted at ensuring that both the platform and the Centre of Excellence are running smoothly, working their way towards the vision and maximising their potential:

- Actively implement and manage Governance across all of the '7 waves'
- Build SharePoint solutions
- Manage relationships with third-party solution providers
- Seek out opportunities for technology innovation that aligns to business vision

- Ensure a constant flow of feedback / continuous improvement / Kaizen activities with the business
- Visualise their work to support transparency, innovation and user adoption.

Roles / Members

The constitution of the SharePoint Centre of Excellence will vary from organisation to organisation depending on its size, the type and scale of SharePoint solutions and of course the organisations SharePoint maturity. For some organisations this will be a virtually capability, for others it will be a full-time team.

Either way it is important that this capability exists and is clearly defined and recognised within your organisation. The Centre of Excellence should include in some way, shape or form at least the following areas:

Technical Authority

The key people in the group who have deep technical and architectural skill in addition to being able to partake in grown-up sensible business conversations.

Subject Matter Experts (SME's)

A range of people with deep skills in specific areas of the technology platform. Examples being, Search, Collaboration, Forms, Records Management, Workflow etc. As always these roles should be able to have grown up sensible business conversations.

Change Agents

Very business focussed people with a broad range of both business skills and high-level SharePoint capability. This role should be able to engage end-users, business stakeholders and executive teams to facilitate business change.

Requirements Facilitators

A new breed of *Business Analyst* that utilise more collaborative, emergent and facilitative techniques, such as collaborative play, Innovation Games and Gamestorming, to engage the business and articulate measurable business outcomes.

End-User Trainers

A role capable of training end-users both on core SharePoint functionality and customised business solutions, as well as playing a fundamental part in all the change management activities.

All these roles should be business facing and 'T'-Shaped i.e. have a broad knowledge across all the roles in the Centre of Excellence and deep knowledge and experience in their specific area of focus.

In some cases it may be appropriate to combine some of these roles such as Technical Authority and SME's or perhaps Change Agents and Requirements Facilitators and End-User Trainers.

However, the SharePoint Centre of Excellence should always be represented as a team with sufficient capability and resource to deliver multiple projects and initiatives as well as continuing their proactive responsibilities.

Organisational Authority

Your SharePoint Centre of Excellence should be, at least for day to day Governance and SharePoint matters, **completely autonomous**.

Let me repeat that...**they should be completely autonomous**.

Typically, the success of a SharePoint Centre of Excellence is largely due to having the right members, a realistic vision, shared understanding and commitment and it being small and autonomous. Although it may seem very disruptive, having a 'band' of SharePoint related people in your organisation, acting in an autonomous manner for the greater good of your organisation, you can find evidence wherever you look that this is in fact an awesome way for you to structure your organisation to work effectively. You can see examples of this in the early days of Visa and in the team-based, flat lattice organisational structure and strong culture (Gore. W, http://bit.ly/LatticeOrg) of W. L. Gore Associates (the creators of GoreTex) among others.

Finally, for this section, on a related topic, based on experience, it is critical that the SharePoint platform has very clear, proactive and transparent executive sponsorship; I see part of the role of the Centre of Excellence being to maintain this sponsorship, support the sponsor and amplify the value.

Where decision making is clearly outside the SharePoint Centre of Excellence remit, there should be a clear and expedient communications route to the Functional and Strategic Governance Boards and where applicable to the executive sponsor if they are outside of the Governance Board structure.

Tummelers

Once again I have to start a section with some words and thoughts about names... Again to be honest I don't care what you call a Tummeler in your organisation:

- Advocate
- Ambassador
- Leader.

But in this instance I really do recommend you use 'Tummeler', why, because it is a word that most people haven't heard of and certainly not used in the context of SharePoint, so using this label will encourage creative friction and prompt people to question and enquire, which can only help with user and stakeholder engagement.

What is a Tummeler?

'Tummel' is a Yiddish word for the person who catalyses others to action; traditionally hired at Jewish weddings to encourage everyone to dance and have fun throughout the whole duration of the wedding party. You could also derive this 'behaviour' from the 'warm-up acts' that are often common-place for comedians or musicians, whose job it is to get the audience in the 'right mood' for the main act.

The word 'Tummel' originates from the German 'tummeln', which means 'to stir'.

A significant challenge we see in a huge number of collaboration platform implementations is that once live, the momentum, user adoption and business value can very quickly bottom out without any on-going stimulus or proactive call to action. In fact without an on-going embedded and sustained stimulus, as far as our collaboration goals go, we will all fall back to our old methods, such as email very quickly.

Anecdotally, it seems that it is typical for the initial buzz of a new platform to plateau and begin to degrade, at around the two to three months period after launch.

Embedding a significant number of SharePoint Tummelers into the business, transparently and proactively supported by the Centre of Excellence described earlier, who can 'be the change' that you want to instil into the organisation, is of huge importance and value.

But what we absolutely must take into consideration and this is perhaps one of those counter-intuitive moments, is that we *cannot and must not* EVER nominate or pressurise, award or allocate Tummelers to their position. Tummelers need to naturally emerge from the business and it is one of the roles of the Centre of Excellence to seek out, identify and then proactively engage with these individuals

By their very nature they need to 'just happen'.

Scope

Tummelers in your organisation should, I hope, be continually using the SharePoint solution both from a technical, organisational and cultural perspective, to its best advantage, becoming key advocates for this new way of working and supporting their colleagues, feeding back to the Centre of Excellence and governance boards, demonstrating value and leading by example.

A judicious use of Tummelers within your organisation is an extremely powerful tool for sustaining business value from your platform investments.

Typically the Centre of Excellence members themselves should also be classed as Tummelers and should be conscious of their interactions with the SharePoint platform and its users to ensure that only positive change and actions are reinforced.

Ant's Tip:

Business Tummelers evolve but YOU need to be the SharePoint 'team' governance Tummeler

Responsibilities

As this is not a formal role, more like a persona or set of values and behaviours, there is no formal set of responsibilities. However, value has been experienced by formally identifying and socialising the Tummelers existence once they have become established and clearly and constantly fulfil the roles needs.

In short, the potential or emergent responsibilities of a Tummeler are as follows:

- Do their day job well
- Have a shared understanding and shared commitment to the platform Vision (though technically every user of the platform should be aligned to this)
- Use the platform effectively to help achieve both the organisation and the platform's goals
- Be advocates for the platform and any associated technologies and solutions e.g. SharePoint
- Maintain transparent and proactive communications with the Centre of Excellence, Governance Structures and Power Users.

Activities

As with the responsibilities mentioned above, there is no real definitive list of activities that a SharePoint Tummeler needs to action in order to 'stay in post'. By definition this would be counter-productive, but some examples of the activities that may be appropriate include:

- Publically demonstrate a shared understanding and shared commitment to the Vision

- Transparently exhibit the relevant change in behaviours
- Communicate openly and regularly with the Centre of Excellence on both positive and negative issues
- Never sending attachments internally within the organisation
- Creating collaborative areas to proactively work with colleagues
- Rating content
- Contributing to discussions
- Proactively helping colleagues
- Participating in Centre of Excellence events
- Creating appropriate content types, metadata etc.
- Correctly utilising metadata (Terms and Keywords) on all content.

Remember, being a SharePoint Tummeler is a way of life, not just for Christmas or SharePoint launch day!

SharePoint Power Users

There is a little less to say about these guys, actually a lot less, especially as I'm being disruptive and not talking about SharePoint the technology platform in what is predominantly a SharePoint book!

Your SharePoint Power Users are the more technology focussed people within the business. They are those people that can **really** be central to the organisations use of SharePoint in solving new business problems and innovating.

These people are likely to be the team or department tinkerers, developing their own solutions to help themselves and their colleagues solve the business and productivity problems.

The challenge is that these are the people that created business critical applications in Access or Excel that weren't supported or scalable and that half the organisation didn't even know existed. They are quite often anti-Tummelers, if there is such a word, who won't use the platform if it doesn't seem like it will help them solve their business problems.

They can, left to their own devices, in some cases, be your worst nightmare!

That said they can also be incredibly powerful, useful and a clear benefit to the organisation, if they are 'steered' in the correct way, and that is your job in the Centre of Excellence.

- Find these people
- Engage with them
- Show them the vision
- Get a shared understanding and commitment
- Support them in their tinkering and innovation.

The reality is that although these people can be either very dangerous or very useful in your organisation, you need them. They can seriously increase the value the business gets from the platform, they can reduce support calls and user problems being escalated and they act as another great sounding board for future kaizen activities for the platform.

What this group of business users really need is 'ying and yang'.

They need very strong, clear Governance to ensure they use the platform appropriately (Ying).

They need a way to play, tinker, innovate, test and break stuff (Yang).

In my experience the best way to do this is to give these SharePoint Power Users access to a 'sand-pit' area via your centrally stored SharePoint Governance content and proactively support their curiosity.

Learn from these people, support them and bring them into the SharePoint Centre of Excellence 'family'.

Process

As you may have gleaned from the Manifesto so far, process isn't something that I hold in strong regard within a SharePoint context and it certainly isn't, from what I have experienced, going to be the saviour of Governance.

Let's be clear, it's not that I don't think that process has a place. Certainly there are many scenarios where processes must be provable under audit for financial, public sector and legal firms for example. But it is more that I think that way too many organisations put a significant emphasis on control, processes and structure for what is in a great deal of situations, a collaborative or social business solution, where rigidity is immensely counter-productive.

That said, there are a few scenarios that are worthy of note and our attention.

Your business users may need a level of structure or some low-key, perhaps even optional processes in order help steer them towards the vision. This is especially true in situations where SharePoint or collaboration maturity is at a very low-level.

There is, quite rightly, a desire to move your business users to be significantly more self sufficient in some areas of SharePoint configuration and administration, but that is for most organisations, the long game. With areas such as new site creation I sometimes recommend clients put in some manual steps as part of the automation while their adoption and maturity is at a low level. These manual steps are important whilst building maturity, as they:

- Build engagement and relationships direct with the business
- Allow you to question the 'Why?' for new sites and new functionality
- Raise awareness of how the Centre of Excellence can support and facilitate the business
- Encourage 'working out loud'

- Increase organisational SharePoint maturity.

As the SharePoint maturity of the business increases then the process can become increasingly automated.

Use processes, structure and formality only where you can definitely see that it supports and facilitates the organisation achieving its Vision.

Always ask the business 'Why?', stop them talking and leading with technology features and steer your organisation, holistically towards your Vision.

In Too Deep?

I've hopefully filled you're head with a range of disruptive thoughts and approaches that you're going to really want to use in your organisation, in this project and the next.

Remember, when it comes to embedding SharePoint Governance into your organisation, make sure your plans are covering:

- Governance Content (Documents)
- Governance Decision Making (Boards)
- In-line Governance (Sign-posting and Steering).

When you are up and running with SharePoint in your business, allow, promote, support and facilitate people going off the rails, give them the comfort and support and places to play. Make sure that you are enabling kaizen within the business, the platform and your team and keep driving SharePoint business value and avoiding SharePoint Celery.

Of course the risk of allowing the business to drive your platform is that they go too far off the rails...

SPLASH!

So, make sure you have lifeguards on station and give all your business users a life-jacket and a GPS...

F.Y.I if that last analogy didn't make sense then I'm basically saying make sure you have a shared understanding and shared commitment across the organisation on your Vision, Governance and YOU!

Governance Survival Kit

Surfboards, post-its, pens & other disruptive tools

For as long as I can remember I have always attributed more value to a conversation than to a process or spread sheet or document. Yes I agree you can't always do without these things, but we really shouldn't be leading with them or using them as a crutch for getting things done.

Analogue, visual, facilitative, fun, engaging, disruptive, they're the attributes of the tools **you** need in the new world.

They may seem alien to you today, but more and more I'm seeing these 'things' appear more and more in everyday business.

I remember smiling to myself when I read the following passages in Howard Schultz's book *'Onward: How Starbucks Fought For Its Life without Losing Its Soul'*. He was talking about what was to be a pivotal Starbucks executive retreat:

> "...someone handed me a black Sharpie, a white iPod, and a packet of index cards."
>
> "..Everyone was deep in thought, but playfully so. The meeting had begun on such a sensory note with the music, the effervescent posters, even the writing with pens instead of keyboards, that it immediately transported our minds to a different place..."

Disrupting the way we work, is key to us making progress in this world and I mean that generally as well as for our technology projects!

You have a new and exciting journey to make now.

Motivated by the epiphany I hope you are currently having, you need to move yourself and your organisation from the status quo towards your Vision.

To do this effectively you need to be armed with a clear Vision and an arsenal of tools to go and sort out your own software projects and the harsh realities of your organisations software project hell.

To make this journey start with the following little steps:

1. Hold a respectful wake for 'Business Analysis'

It's not their fault they're dead, the world just moved on and even we didn't notice, but raise a glass for us while you're there

2. De-wax your ears

You're going to have to listen a whole lot more, I said YOU'RE GOING TO HAVE... Oh forget it!

3. Never be more than 5 feet away from a whiteboard or a large piece of paper

How else will you communicate? Pens my friend (and a board rubber)

4. Stop reading techie books

Well at least read a lot less than you used to. Technical books and a deep understanding of SharePoint's technbical complexity is of course important, but we can learn a hell of a lot more from non-IT books than just looking at the comforting bedtime stories of server farm maintenance.

I've started to compile a list of my recommended non-techie books to read in the following blog post: http://bit.ly/NoMoreTechieBooks

5. Write less words

Except for this book I hope, which was meant to be a lot more visual than it turned out, no-one wants to read lots of stuff written down on paper anymore, period.

6. Draw more pictures

Sketches, visualisations, collaborations, infographics, pictures, doodles are way more effective at passing knowledge than the blah blah

blah in Word documents, PowerPoint, PDF or Excel.

7. Play with yourself (stop sniggering) and your business

Learn about play, games, gamification, game mechanics for these are your differentiator in this brave new world.

Awesome!

Now we are making progress, how does it feel?

Seriously, you're changing the way you are working and perceiving the SharePoint world, tell me what it feels like... (http://bit.ly/TalkToSoulsailor)

Cool tools

Here's a selection of what I think are some of the essential tools. This selection is based on my experience, mistakes and what I have learnt in the dark underbelly of SharePoint projects.

These tools will really help you get Governance working effectively in your organisation and sustain your momentum towards that Vision...

Now when you finish the book, it won't be too long now, I want you to go out and beg, borrow, steal, make and create your own Governance toolkit, to help you steer your organisation and SharePoint platform...

Here is some of the stuff you need to get your hands on:

This Manifesto

OK so you already have a version of this, hopefully not stolen! But it might make sense to get a few more copies for your colleagues and the business stakeholders

A Surfboard

Maybe you don't need an actual surfboard, albeit that would be pretty cool. But what you do need is the tools and mechanisms to track your progress towards the vision.

Rory's Story Cubes

These are cool facilitation tools; you've seen them already in the Visual Thesis section. They are basically a set of dice with visual images on each face which you can use to construct a story. The product page is here: http://www.storycubes.com

I use them with my kids to create fun little stories and I've used them with customers as ice-breakers or to facilitate people explaining their requirements, vision and new concepts.

All credit to Joe Capka (http://jcapka.blogspot.co.uk) for introduc-
ing me to them in a great little bar in Utrecht at a training course I
was running.

A HUGE Roll of Paper

Whatever you are doing, you'll probably want to get it down on
paper. This is some hard-core paper. Basically it's large format
printer paper, on a roll.

I use: HP Coated bond paper (bright white) on a roll (84.1 cm x 45.7
m) - 90 g/m2 ordered from Amazon:

http://bit.ly/BigAssPaperRoll

It's pretty thick, so most (not all) pens don't bleed through it. I've
covered tables with it to allow people to doodle and sketch thoughts
and ideas and stuck it to walls. Get yourself one of those 'artist'
telescopic tubes to carry it around in.

Why do I bother, well mainly because I find in a lot of cases, clients
don't have the *right* kit for facilitating, small whiteboards, one pen
and someones stolen the whiteboard rubber! With this and other
items I've listed you become self-sufficient and it's one less thing to
worry about when really all you really want to do is draw a huge
sketch of 7 waves and run an audit session...

Magic Whiteboard

This is an awesome alternative or addition to lugging a huge roll of
paper around.

These are re-usable sheets, on a roll, of electrostatic, stick-like-shit-
to-a-blanket mini whiteboards. Mega useful for running ad-hoc
workshops in non-facilitator-friendly locations. Get some because
you will need them!

http://bit.ly/ConsultantsFriend

Governance Framework

Whether or not you agree with the '7 waves of SharePoint Governance' you need to have some kind of structured approach to delivering and sustaining Governance in your organisation.

Make sure you have something to rely on...

Camera

The fact of the matter is that:

- Post-it's fall off
- Pens smudge and fade
- Context can be lost.

You will find very quickly that photos of sketches, facilitation sessions and any other workshop assets are a valuable commodity.

Preserve them in images or video. They add a significant weight and added dimension to documentation.

I use my iPhone or a GoPro Hero 3 (http://gopro.com).

Posters

Using a graphic canvas, frameworks or a poster of some sorts can be a great way to frame and steer a Governance workshop. Whether you use pre-built templates from people like David Sibbet's (Grove Consultants International http://www.grove.com) or something you created or even getting the workshop participants to create a graphic framework themselves; these are all very useful and powerful tools for ensuring that your workshops achieve a positive outcome and generate valuable insights.

Remember you want to be working out loud!

Stories

Listen to stories.

Tell stories.

Collect stories.

Why? Emotional connection, insights, value and engagement

We are hard-wired for storytelling, whether it is audio or visual, stories are extremely powerful and valuable.

Innovation Games

These are a set of awesome facilitation techniques, designed by Luke Hohmann and articulated in the book by the same name (http://bit.ly/InnovGamesBook).

Born out of 'product management', these techniques are fantastic for facilitating positive outcomes from your workshops, enabling you in an engaging way, gain clear insights into stakeholders requirements, prioritise, visualise, explore and define as well as a host of other benefits.

My favourite techniques include:

- Sailboat
- Hot Tub
- Product Box
- Prune the Product Tree.

Gamestorming

In a similar vein, but released later a few years after Innovation Games, this book unleashes a huge and ever growing, array of what I call 'Collaborative Play' techniques that can be used for visual/analogue facilitation.

My favourite technique has to be *Cover Story*.

Check them out, try them and create your own...

Drawing Sticks

Sketching, doodling, drawing, white boarding are all skills that you should try to improve to help embed and sustain your SharePoint Governance.

Remember that 'good enough' is most definitely good enough.

Ant's Tip:

When I'm practicing sketching, my test for 'good enough' is asking my 5 year old daughter what I've drawn, if she gets it right then its good enough!

It doesn't matter what type or make you use, here's a sample of what is in my pencil case:

- Copic Sketch
- Copic Multiliner
- Pencil
- Pencil Crayon
- Pentel Brush
- Chalk
- Sharpie
- Pentel Energel 0.7mm.

Explore and experiment as there is a HUGE world of pens and related instruments out there. Depending on what you are doing, your clients and your own personality there will be a style and a sketching instrument for you... and if there isn't then you can always try these alternatives:

- Play Dough
- Lego
- Craft material.

But don't forget, in the infamous words of 'Musical Youth' in 1982:

"...Pass the Dutchie on the left hand side..."

What I mean is, don't hog the pens and materials, pass them to your customer, client, stakeholder, users and get them to do some of the work for you.

Lead the way, then let them go and listen and watch carefully for the insights to really flow.

Happiness

Have I gone too far again?

The way I see things is that engaging in a workshop, helping clients define their vision, embedding Governance in an organisation, helping clients steer SharePoint to success is a positive and very valuable activity.

You are delivering value and enabling potentially significant business gain and opportunity for your organisation or your clients. That's something to be proud of and happy about.

Smile.

Joke.

Laugh.

Enjoy the process.

It's infectious.

It's positive.

Technology

No matter how hard I try I can't get more than 100 feet away from technology in my projects and that includes SharePoint Governance engagements.

Ant's Tip:

Don't depend on technology for your Governance salvation, because that won't help you.

But...

Technology or rather technology Governance tools can play a useful part.

I'm not going to write much, because you guys are more than capable of researching tool vendors and finding one that suits; however to steer you in the right direction, here's a few avenues that I would definitely look at (in no order of preference:

- Axceler
- Avepoint
- Codeplex (Not a vendor and please approach with caution!)
- MetaVis
- Etc.

Tell 'em I sent you!

Art and Craft Materials

More and more I'm finding that a workshop or meeting with no analogue component is a **FAIL**.

Allowing yourself and the participants to hide behind their devices, PowerPoint, projector screen etc. is counter productive.

When I say analogue component, what I mean is some element that involves people doing stuff... Standing up, moving around, sketching, moving post-it notes about, playing twister, building product boxes, mime, interpretive dance, whatever get's the attendees actually physically engaging in the process.

Whether you use a whiteboard or a graphic template or immerse your attendees in art and craft materials probably doesn't matter, but use something to engage, excite and encourage the emergent thoughts and ideas.

When I say arts and craft materials I am being serious, I have a large box full of all sorts of things that I user for activities such as 'Cover Story' or 'Product Box' or just general facilitation sessions. In my mind the crazier the materials the greater opportunity for use, innovation and awesome insights:

- Pipe Cleaners
- Glitter Glue
- Google Eyes
- Stickers
- Post-Its
- Lollipop Sticks
- Furry Balls
- Plastic Charms
- Pens (see above)
- Foam Shapes.

Go wild!

There's some examples of workshops in action on the website http://bit.ly/SoulSailorInAction

Sketchbook

I always carry a sketchbook around with me now, whether it's to use to help articulate a concept to someone in a one-on-one, or to jot down insights in a workshop or ideas in the park it's very useful to have a quick and easy way of capturing stuff.

Autodesk SketchBook Pro

This is my tool of choice for sketches that I want to include in documents or Governance content.

SketchBook Pro is a great tool for creating hand drawn diagrams and sketches on your tablet. For the really talented you can actually create beautiful drawings, for the likes of me you can achieve 'good enough'.

I quite often use it to sketch out concepts, ideas and to try to refine how I articulate new concepts to clients.

It can also act as an effective whiteboard replacement when connected to a projector.

If you have a tablet / slate type device then you need to buy it today...

It ROCKS!

Bad workshops can kill

Well maybe not quite, but a poorly run session can really hamper your Governance progress.

There are a huge number of books and courses and content out there that can help you facilitate workshops more effectively.

Here's a random selection of my top tips for more effective Governance workshops:

1. Prepare more than you think you should and be workshop-ready before the attendees arrive, it takes more time than you think to set-up for an effective facilitation session
2. Always, always start with a Vision
3. Be strong with the client when requesting attendees; it's essential that you have good business representation and the right people at the workshop to get the desired outcome
4. Try not to run a workshop with less than 6 people (ideally 8+)
5. If you have a large group (12+) then draft in more facilitators
6. Splitting the attendees into two or more groups of 4+ is really effective
7. Variety is the spice of life and having mixed groups from across the business in most situations is most effective
8. Be careful of the HIPPO; don't let the **HI**ghest **P**aid **P**erson's **O**pinion override everyone else
9. Be as visual as you can
10. Be positive, conversational, helpful and facilitative
11. Listen
12. Listen again
13. Capture both the details of the activity and the emergent conversations and behaviours
14. The room, layout, arrangement of tables and chairs matters
15. Keep an eye on the clock, be punctual, have regular breaks and don't overrun

16. Relax, breathe, smile, breathe, be confident, breathe...

If you bare these in mind then hopefully your workshops won't suck!

Ant's Tip:

Use an informal layout with circular tables such as 'cabaret' to make the most out of your workshop and remember you will need a much bigger room than you think!.

Post-It Note Psychology

To end this section on your Governance Survival Kit, I'd like to take a few moments to make you aware of the importance of the psychology of Post-It Notes.

To be more exact it's the psychology of *placing* these sticky little innovators on a wall that I want to share with you.

Disclaimer: I am no psychologist

I've noticed over the years that an organisations culture emerges in plain sight when you combine:

- Whiteboard (or any other surface)
- Diverse stakeholder group
- Sticky Notes
- A goal or question.

I'm not going to go into lots of detail or prove this to you in any way, that's not the purpose of this Manifesto, but it's an intriguing area that I think you should be aware within your organisation.

In your Governance workshops, when you're faced with an activity that involves sticky notes, be aware of the behaviours around you and ask yourself some of these questions:

- How are the sticky notes being arranged - Group think, consensus, HIPPO?
- Is anyone moving everyone elses sticky notes? Signs of domination, request they don't
- Is anyone covering up other sticky notes with theirs? Are they aggressive, domineering, a HIPPO?
- Are people questioning what's written on the sticky notes? This could lead to valuable emergent insights, context, background information, cultural differences, new avenues to explore

- Who is using the pink sticky notes or the odd-shaped ones? Maybe they are creative people or are they trying to highlight specific points
- Who is generating lots of sticky notes, who is generating very few?
- Ask people to explain their sticky notes. Are people in agreement, disagreement, ambivalent?
- Is someone sticking-with-force? Why are they doing this?
- Think about where and how people are placing their sticky notes, what hidden meaning is there, if any?

In my opinion, those little square sticky things can reveal much more about the business culture of your organisation in a one hour facilitation session, than a HIPPO Consultant could derive in a very expensive weeks work.

Think about it in the next workshop you are in, what does the sticky notes behaviour reveal?

Apres Sail

Is this really the end?

"However beautiful the strategy, you should occasionally look at the results." - Sir Winston Churchill

Oh crap, this is the last bit of the book, what should I say to end this Manifesto in the right way?

Maybe I should just stop mid-sentence, maybe I should shut-up now?

There's no heroine or hero that conquers all, or maybe there is and it's you?

There's no love lost or found, but perhaps you've re-kindled your love for a business approach to SharePoint?

No treasure, although perhaps the treasure is the progress you make towards the Vision?

No battle to be won, except perhaps against those technology led approaches to SharePoint Governance. *Let's face it out of everything else discussed in this Manifesto, this is a key point. Turn your SharePoint projects into business change projects and you're on the path to victory!*

No mystery to unfold, but maybe the early parts of this Manifesto did in-fact clarify the mystery behind failed approaches to SharePoint Governance?

Finally, there was no cliff-hanger, or was there... Nope, I don't plan (today) to write another edition, I'm handing this story over to you to finish in your own words.

Retrospective

I guess there are one or two things that haven't been said, some thoughts around SharePoint Governance that perhaps need reiterating or reinforcing. I'm sure there will be things I've forgotten to say, concepts that I could have explained better and maybe even a few final subversive undertones that might just surface before the very end.

This book has taken much longer than expected to write.

I am really sorry about that!

This book is less visual than I wanted.

That's a disappointment for me, but it's the way the book emerged and I'm comfortable with that.

This book has more knowledge and experience in it than I realised I ever had.

That was a real surprise to me!

I have loved writing this Manifesto.

I am proud to bring **disruptive Governance thinking to the masses**.

I want to thank you before we part company, for being part of this journey, now right at the start and also in the future as we head towards our many visions.

But this has never really been about what I think or say or do.

With this Manifesto I wanted to inspire you to change your SharePoint world.

> **The question is..**
>
> **Has this Manifesto changed your SharePoint world?**
>
> **Has it disrupted your Governance thinking?**

I bloody hope so in at least some small way...

Disruption lives here

Governance has a stigma. In quite a few organisations so does SharePoint.

It's a tough job for a lot of us trying to implement Governance, it probably feels like we've been blown out the water before we even start.

But we must start, we will try and we can make a difference.

I hope that you avoid wasting hundreds of thousands of pounds, dollars, euros or whatever implementing a platform that no-one uses...

I hope that you hit the jackpot and deliver huge amounts of business value and bring joy to your projects and organisation...

Whatever we do, we need to deliver, we need to try and we need to play that first note. SharePoint Governance is a lot like **jazz music**. It can be frenetic, full of improvisation, joy, unstructured but artistic.

But jazz is not for everyone, ask my wife Claire.

Just like Governance isn't taken seriously by many in our organisations, in fact it probably isn't even taken seriously enough by lots of our peers in the SharePoint world!

But that needs to change now.

Everyone in the SharePoint world needs to take Governance seriously.

Dirigi in finem

That's Latin for *"To steer to the end."*

And we have finally reached the end of this Manifesto.

My final words, stolen from Seth Godin's book 'Poke the Box', will be very simple and disruptive in whatever context you wish to apply them:

> *"Please stop waiting for a map."*
>
> *"We reward those who draw maps, not those who follow them."*

Now go and draw your own map

References

All the links within this book can be found in the following bit.ly bundle: *http://bit.ly/LinkBundle_SPGovManifesto*

Adaptive Capacity, [Online], *http://en.wikipedia.org/wiki/Adaptive_capacity*

Collins, J. & Jerry, P., 1994. *Big Hairy Audacious Goal.* [Online], *http://bit.ly/BigHairyAudaciousGoal*

Covey, Stephen R., 2000. *7 Habits of Highly Effective People.* Available at: *http://bit.ly/Coveys7Habits*

Culmsee, P., 2012. *Clever Workarounds.* [Online]. Available at *http://bit.ly/Culmsee*

Field of Dreams. 1989. [Film]. Directed by Phil Alden Robinson.

Foley, M. J., 2011. *All About Microsoft.* [Online]. Available at: *http://bit.ly/SharePointMomentum*

Gray, D., Brown, S., Macanufo, J., 2010. *Gamestorming.* O'Reilly. Available at: *http://bit.ly/GamestormingGovernance*

Godin, S., 2011. *Poke the Box.* The Domino Project. Available at: *http://bit.ly/PokeSeth*

Gore, W., *A Team-Based, Flat Lattice Organization.* [Online]. Available at: *http://bit.ly/LatticeOrg*

Heifetz, R., 2009. *Practice of Adpative Leadership.* Harvard Business School Press. Available at: *http://bit.ly/AdaptiveHeifetz*

Hinchcliffe, D., Kim, P., 2012. *Social Business By Design: Transformative Social Media Strategies for the Connected Company.* Jossey Bass. Available at: *http://bit.ly/SocialByDesign*

Hohmann, L, 2006. *Innovation Games.* Addison Wesley. Available at: *http://bit.ly/InnovGamesBook*

Kleon, A., 2012. *Steal Like an Artist.* Workman. Available at: *http://bit.ly/StealItAll*

Locke, C., Levine, R., Searls, D. & Weinberger, D., 2000. *The Clutrain Manifesto: The end of business as usual.* Perseus Books. Available at: *http://bit.ly/TheCluetrainManifesto*

Marshall, B.,*Rightshifting.* [Online]. Available at:

http://bit.ly/MarshallModel

Osterwalder, A., Pigneur, Y., 2010. *Business Model Generation: A Handbook for Visionaries, Game Changers, and Challengers.* John Wiley & Sons. Available at: *http://bit.ly/SharePointBusinessModel*

Pink, D., 2011 *Drive.* Canongate Books Ltd. Available at: *http://bit.ly/PinkBookDrive*

Pretor-Pinney, G., 2011 *The WaveWatchers Companion.* Bloomsbury Paperbacks. Available at: *http://bit.ly/WaveWatcher*

Ries, E., 2011. *The Lean Startup: How Constant Innovation Creates Radically Successful Businesses.* Portfolio Penguin. Available at: *http://bit.ly/LeanStartupSharePoint*

Rittel, P. H., 2012. *Wicked Problem.* [Online]. Available at: *http://bit.ly/WickedProblem*

Schultz, H., 2011. *Onward: How Starbucks Fought For Its Life Without Losing Its Soul.* John Wiley & Sons. Available at: *http://bit.ly/SavingStarbucksSoul*

Senge, P., 1994. *Learning Organisation.* [Online]

http://en.wikipedia.org/wiki/Learning_organization

Senge, P., 2006. *The Fifth Discipline.* Random House Business. Available at: *http://bit.ly/SengeThinking*

Sinek, S., 2009. *How great leaders inspire action* [Online]. Available at: *http://bit.ly/Sinek-why*

Sinek, S., 2011. *Start With Why*. Penguin. Available at: *http://bit.ly/Sinek-Why-Book*

Snowden, D., 2012. *Wikipedia - Cynefin.* [Online]. Available at: *http://bit.ly/Cynefin*

Williams, B., 2010. *When will we Work Out Loud? Soon!* [Online]. Available at: *http://bit.ly/WorkOutLoud*

The Standish Group, 1995. *The Chaos Report.* The Standish Group. [Online]. Available at: *http://bit.ly/ChaosReport*

Who are Soulsailor Consulting?

Soulsailor Consulting Ltd (http://www.SoulsailorConsulting.com) is a micro-consultancy, established early in 2012 by Ant Clay (http://uk.linkedin.com/in/antonyclay). We are focussed on enabling organisational value by positively disrupting your technology projects.

We work extensively with our clients and partner organisations to align their people and technology investments to organisational outcomes, whilst changing the way that they work through facilitation, visualisation, collaborative play and organisational storytelling.

We regularly deliver consultancy, coaching, training, workshops and speaks on a range of technology and organisational change topics including:

- Governance
- Requirements facilitation
- Workshop and meeting facilitation
- Collaboration projects (SharePoint, Yammer, Office365 etc.)
- Gamification strategy
- Social business
- Change management.

Feel free to get in touch (http://bit.ly/TalkToSoulsailor) if you think your technology projects need positively disrupting!

12399116R00120

Printed in Great Britain
by Amazon.co.uk, Ltd.,
Marston Gate.